New England's Ghost Towns, Cemeteries, and Memorials

Gone But Not Forgotten

SUMMER PARADIS | CATHY MCMANUS

Schiffer Publishing Ltd

4880 Lower Valley Road • Atglen, PA 19310

Schiffer Books are available at special discounts for bulk purchases for sales promotions or premiums. Special editions, including personalized covers, corporate imprints, and excerpts can be created in large quantities for special needs. For more information contact the publisher:

Published by Schiffer Publishing, Ltd.
4880 Lower Valley Road
Atglen, PA 19310
Phone: (610) 593-1777; Fax: (610) 593-2002
E-mail: Info@schifferbooks.com.

For the largest selection of fine reference books on this and related subjects, please visit our website at www.schifferbooks.com.
We are always looking for people to write books on new and related subjects. If you have an idea for a book, please contact us at
proposals@schifferbooks.com.

This book may be purchased from the publisher.
Please try your bookstore first.
You may write for a free catalog.

Designed by RoS
Type set in GodOfWar/Adobe Jenson

ISBN: 978-0-7643-4552-4
Printed in China

DEDICATION

To our family and friends for all your continued support and to our fellow New Englanders for your unfailing hospitality to us during our travels. We are constantly reminded why New England is such a special part of the country to call home.

ACKNOWLEDGMENTS

This book would not have been possible without the support of all our family and friends and those who encouraged and helped us along the way. A special thank you to Mike Dauphin for being our boat captain and helping us fulfill our dream of making it to Malaga Island and to Katie and Beckah Boyd for their constant advice, support, and friendship.

Summer –

For my one true love, my amazing son, Jacob Parsons. You are my everything. Also a huge "Thank You" to my parents, Bob and Karin Langdon Paradis, for understanding why writing is so important to me and removing any and all obstacles to make this book come together. I hope I've made you proud.

Cathy –

Thanks to my family for all their support. My parents, Jim and Claudette McManus, who not only encouraged me but even traveled with me to a few locations and shared some great stories with me. Thanks to David and Lora McManus, Dan McManus and Kim Lagasse – you guys are awesome. For Matt and James McManus, in you I see the best of both your parents. The two of you inspire me to be a better person. Thanks to my extended family, all my cousins, uncles and aunts. Together, we make the best group of weirdos in the world.

Finally, I want to thank all of our friends and followers online, primarily FaceBook; the ideas and support you provided helped us in more ways than I can say.

CONTENTS

1
AMERICA'S STONEHENGE
Salem, New Hampshire

This site also demonstrates one of the great dangers of archaeology; not to life and limb, although that does sometimes take place. I'm talking about folklore.

~INDIANA JONES

Just a few miles north of Salem, New Hampshire, lies the remains of a settlement from about 4,000 years ago. The site, now called America's Stonehenge, has a series of stone structures spread out over 30 acres. The site is fascinating; you have old stone structures that have been built from the rocks that litter the terrain. There is a giant, astronomically aligned calendar that spans over 20 acres of this New Hampshire woodlands. The calendar has strategically placed stones that line up with events, such as the Equinox Sunrise, the Winter and Summer Solstice, etc. There is even a huge sacrificial table with a groove carved around the edge to drain blood away. Set up nearby, the sacrificial stone is an oracle chamber, a hidden room set up like an echo chamber, so that during ceremonies someone could be hidden away from sight to create a disembodied voice that wafted up from under the table.

No one knows who lived at this settlement or why the area was deserted, but in 1937, it was given a new purpose. William Goodwin, an insurance company executive and amateur archeologist, purchased the land and began excavating the site. Goodwin believed that Irish Cudlee Monks had come across the Atlantic around 4,000 years ago and created the site. He thought that the building structures and stone placements were reminiscent of architecture from Bronze Age Europe. Unfortunately, in his exuberance over his find, he "fixed" the placement of some of the stones to match with what he believed the site had been. So, we can't truly know what was at the site originally, thus throwing into doubt Goodwin's findings.

Above from left:
The Sacrificial Table. A groove around the outside edge is rumored to have carried bodily fluids off of the rock.

Site 13. A former home site with a lilac bush planted on the roof.

Stone walls and cellar holes at America's Stonehenge.

Opposite:
Large stone slabs at America's Stonehenge

Curtis Runnels, a CAS professor of archaeology, does not believe that America's Stonehenge was built by the Celts in ancient time. There have been no finds of Bronze Age artifacts that European settlers would have used. As runnels said:

> The whole point of having a specialized science such as archaeology is that we've determined certain methods of figuring out how we know what we know. If you have a Bronze Age site in, say, Great Britain, near Stonehenge, ... you're going to find artifacts of bronze, tin, copper, gold and silver, and they will have distinct forms that are easily recognized....They haven't found anything like this. I'm just an old fashioned empirical archaeologist. I want to see evidence.

Many archeologists believe the stones on the site have been left by local farmers in the 18th and 19th centuries. Even the sacrificial stone table has been questioned. The grooves carved into the stone resemble lye-leaching stones that many farms in the area used to extract lye from wood ashes to make soap.

So, the two sides disagree with what the site was and who lived there, but they do agree that it was once a settlement either of ancient European visitors or of a Native American Tribe. Whichever side you choose to believe, one thing is certain: The area, once known as Mystery Hill, is still a mystery for us today.

AUTHOR NOTES

We visited America's Stonehenge in early August and it was an incredibly hot and humid day – one of those days when you feel like you have a wet towel draped over you; and the bugs were out in full force. Despite that, we had a great time. We started out in the Visitor's Center, where we watched a brief video about the site, then we were given a map of the site and set off to explore. No matter who built this site, it is fascinating to walk around and examine all the formations or to crawl around in the dark cave – especially nice since it was about 20 degrees cooler in the caves and a break from the heat.

The site is also reportedly haunted and there are occasionally nighttime investigations that the public can attend. We had no paranormal experiences, but being able to wander the site as part of a nighttime investigation is definitely on my bucket list now.

We spoke with Dennis in the Visitor's Center; he was friendly and knowledgeable about the site and very enthusiastic about sharing stories. We would recommend a visit to anyone in the area – especially for the Alpacas they have on site. Everyone loves Alpacas!

~Summer and Cathy

VISITORS' INFORMATION

America's Stonehenge is located at 105 Haverhill Road in Salem, New Hampshire. There is plenty of free parking on site. Allot plenty of time to wander the grounds and be sure to visit the resident Alpacas.

Right:
Dark and dank rooms.

Below from left:
An underground tunnel built piece-by-piece from small hunks of local granite.

The stone structures were carefully placed.

A covered walkway.

2
SALEM
WITCH TRIAL MEMORIAL
Salem, Massachusetts

"What evil spirit have you familiarity with?"
"None."
"Have you made no contact with the devil?"
"No."
"Why do you hurt these children?"
"I do not hurt them. I scorn it."
"Who do you employ then to do it?"
"I employ no body."
"What creature do you employ then?"
"No creature. I am falsely accused."

~Dialogue based on the examination of
Sarah Good by Judges Hathorne and Corbin

It is a story well-documented and a part of any elementary school curriculum. In 1692, fourteen women and six men were accused of being witches, were tried and convicted. Beginning with Bridget Bishop on June 10th and concluding with Ann Pudeatorm, Wilmott Read, Samuel Wardwell, Margaret Scott, Martha Corey, and Mary Easty on September 22nd – all were executed. A dark time punctuated by hysteria and a corrupt judicial system, the witch trials remain, to this day, a shining example of the dangers of intolerance and the need for due process.

Above from left:
Giles Corey, pressed to death, September 19, 1692 – the 80-year-old man had failed to submit to a trial.

Sarah Good, hanged July 19, 1692.

Bridget Bishop, hanged June 10, 1692 – "I am no witch. I am innocent. I know nothing of it."

Opposite:
A view of the Salem Witch Trial Memorial as seen from within the neighboring Old Burying Point.

Designed by Maggie Smith and James Cutler, following an international competition that garnered 246 entries, the memorial was dedicated in August of 1992. Twenty granite benches inscribed with the names of the victims are cantilevered into a low wall that surrounds the next-door Old Burying Point, Salem's oldest cemetery. Each indicates the date and method of execution. This quiet spot to sit and reflect has been visited by over six million visitors since it's installation.

VISITORS' INFORMATION

The Salem Witch Trial Memorial is located at 98 New Liberty Street in Salem, Massachusetts. While in the area, you may wish to see its companion memorial, the Salem Village Witchcraft Victims' Memorial, at 176 Hobart Street in Danvers.

Clockwise from above:
Low stone benches provide a place to sit and reflect on the atrocity of the trials.

Landscaping surrounding the Salem Witch Trial Memorial adds a calming influence.

Colonial era charm at the Salem Witch Trial Memorial.

Opposite:
Long stone walls interspersed with engraved benches.

3

Irish Famine Memorial

Boston, Massachusetts

We have always found the Irish a bit odd. They refuse to be English.

~Winston Churchill

The stranger reaps our harvest, the alien owns our soil.

~Lady Jane Wilde

From 1845 through 1852, Ireland was going through a time of mass starvation; disease ran rampant, and those who could, fled their home country just to survive. This was the Great Famine or a *Gorta Mòr*, meaning a Great Hunger, and during this time, Ireland lost approximately one quarter of its population. One million people died and another million emigrated; and yet, during this time of famine, food was still being exported.

Since it was illegal in the 17th and 18th centuries for Irish Catholics, eighty percent of the population, to own property, they had no choice but to live on small parcels of land owned by English landlords. They spent the majority of their time working the land for these landlords, and they had little time to work their small allotment of land. Money was so scarce, and the rents, for even the most meager home, were so high, there was little that they could grow to keep their families fed. While the landowners' fields were growing grain crops, the only thing most of the natives could grow were potatoes, this being an easily maintained and obtained crop that needed less space to grow. So the potato became the primary food source for the poor in Ireland.

Then the potato blight hit Ireland. This was not the first time that the potato crops had been destroyed or seriously damaged, and this fungus did not only affect Ireland. The same blight infected most of Europe and parts of America, but with about three million of Ireland's populace being dependent on the potato crop for survival, they were hardest hit.

For those who could, emigration seemed to be the only choice. This, however, was not an easy solution. Not only did they have to leave friends, family, and country behind, but they also had to survive the journey. Approximately one in five passengers died during the trip to North America. There was such a mass exodus from Ireland to America that, by 1850, the populations of Boston, Massachusetts; New York City, New York; Philadelphia, Pennsylvania; and Baltimore, Maryland were twenty-five percent Irish.

The Irish influence is still strongly felt in Boston, Massachusetts, and on June 28, 1998, the Irish Famine Memorial was dedicated to commemorate the 150th anniversary of the Famine. It is on a small patch of land at the corner of Washington and School Streets, just across

Above from left:
An Irish family falls prey to the famine and begins to slowly die of starvation.

A mother in grief over watching her children starve, calls out to the heavens above for divine intervention.

Having arrived in Boston, the family has outlived the Famine and is well nourished and healthy again.

Arrival in the New World.

from the Old South Meeting House. There are two statues, each of three people, surrounded by rock walls with a flat area on top for seating, and there are eight plaques circling the area. In the center, on the ground, is a circular plaque with a map of Ireland and the East Coast of America with a ship sailing towards Boston.

The first statue depicts the suffering Irish: a man, woman, and child, all painfully emaciated. They are difficult to view. The second statue is a representation of the Irish after coming to America. It is of a man, woman, and child looking healthy and fit. There is pride and strength in the attitude of these three. The plaques surrounding the statues are labeled: "Lest We Forget," "Dying of Hunger," "An Gorta Mor," "Boston Sends Help," "The People Were Gaunt," "Crossing the Bowl of Tears," "Arriving in Boston," and "The American Dream." These plaques chronicle not only the hardships faced in Ireland and crossing the sea to get to American, but also touches the struggles and prejudice faced by the newcomers. For, while the people of Boston were willing to send help to the starving of Ireland, it was much different to have thousands of starving, ill people taking up residence and flooding the job market.

This memorial is one of the most controversial in Boston as of 2012. While most people are pleased that there is a monument commemorating the Irish Famine, there are many who dislike the actual monument. The statue of three starving people is the main issue. Art critic Greg Cook runs a website for The New England Journal of Aesthetic Research (http://gregcookland.com/journal/). He invites people to nominate the worst public art in New England. The Boston Irish Famine Memorial is one of his top nominees. According to Cook, the list of complaints received includes: "Simple-minded, facile, maudlin, utterly appalling and embarrassing, poorly executed, the most-cheesy memorial to human tragedy in Boston." Others, however, are not as offended by the depiction and find it a moving and fitting representation of a tragic event.

We would recommend going to see the memorial and decide for yourself – especially since The New England Journal of Aesthetic Research intends to petition the City of Boston, if the Boston memorial is top nominee, to remove the "winner" of their poll and replace it with a more appealing installation.

4
MARY NASSON
Old York, Maine

In the beautiful seaside town of Old York, Maine, sits the Old Burying Yard. Though it is located along Route One, one of the busiest roads in the state, it is a peaceful collection of plots from the sixteen and seventeen hundreds. These are not the final resting places of religious or government officials, but the family plots of everyday citizens.

What you may not expect, as you meander through the rows of leaning stones, is that this is the site of one of Maine's oldest Urban Legends. Mary Nasson was a young housewife living in Old York in the mid-1700s. An herbalist by trade, she earned a meager wage by creating tinctures and elixirs to ease the ailments of her neighbors. She was also said to have provided relief from the "Evil Eye" and performed exorcisms when the need arose. Though some were grateful for her services, these practices were looked upon with great skepticism and cause for concern within the Christian community. Though witch hunts and hysteria had died out considerably in the years before her birth, she was widely considered to be a witch and her behaviors viewed with suspicion.

When she passed away in August of 1774, at the age of 29, her husband, Samuel, commissioned a headstone and footstone to adorn her grave in the Old Burying Yard. Elaborate for the time, the headstone featured an engraving of Mary's likeness followed by a loving epitaph (as shown on the stone).

HERE LIES QUITE FREE FROM LIFES
DISTRESSING CARE,
A LOVING WIFE, A TENDER PARENT DEAR,
CUT DOWN IN MIDST OF DAYS, AS YOU MAY SEE,
BUT- STOP- MY GRIEF, I SOON SHALL EQUAL BE,
WHEN DEATH SHALL STOP MY BREATH,
AND END MY TIME,
GOD GRANT MY DIST, MAY MINGLE, THEN,
WITH THINE

SACRED TO THE MEMORY OF MRS. MARY
NASSON, WIFE OF MR SAMUEL NASSON, WHO
DEPARTED THIS LIVE ON AUG 18TH 1774, AE 29

What made Mary's final resting place so unique, and certainly piqued the villagers' ire, was a large "wolf stone" placed above the casket at ground level. Though Samuel claimed that this stone was intended to keep cattle, pigs, and other animals from disturbing his wife's grave, many in town claimed that it was from his desire to hinder any attempts to dig up the coffin and exorcise the demons in the "witch's" body. Some records indicate that he had plans to relocate to nearby Sanford, Maine, and desired the plot to be easier to maintain. Regardless, Mary's grave is easily distinguishable from any other grave in the cemetery or in the local area.

Above:
Mary Nasson's final resting place with a visible "wolf stone" that is said to radiate heat.

Opposite:
The tombstone of Mary Nasson. Mary Nasson's tombstone features a tympanum with a depiction of Mary on it.

An Urban Legend is Born

As is often the case with unique tombstones, "The Witch's Grave" quickly developed notoriety and began to spread as an urban legend. The rumor mill churned and the cemetery was quickly labeled as haunted and the wolf stone was said to radiate heat. Large crows seen in the vicinity of the Old Burying Yard were regarded as "familiars," supernatural entities thought to aid a witch in her magical dark arts.

Mary's plot fast became the most frequently visited in the Yard, even more so than the victims of the Candlemas Massacre, also interred there, so much so that the Old York Historical Society included the tale on a plaque installed at the location.

AUTHOR NOTES

On the bright and sunny May afternoon that we traveled to the cemetery, we easily spotted Mary's grave on the right-hand side of the cemetery. Though we brought equipment to evaluate claims of the tombstone radiating heat, we were unable to notice any such changes. We did observe that the headstone was made out of slate and the wolf stone was made out of granite, which could conceivably result in the temperature discrepancies that have been reported. Though we felt the cemetery was peaceful and calm, we did observe several large crows wandering around the land which just may have been Mary's "familiars" still paying tribute.

~Summer

VISITORS' INFORMATION

The Old York Burying Yard is located at the corner of Route 1A/York Street and Lindsey Road. On-street parking is often available. It is a short and easy walk from the quaint downtown area if you would like to explore the town before or after you stop to pay your respects to Mrs. Nasson.

5

MONSON CENTER GHOST TOWN
Milford, New Hampshire

Monson Center was an early colonial British settlement in present-day Milford, New Hampshire. With a peak in population in 1767 of 293 individuals, the town covered over 17,000 acres and was initially part of Massachusetts. The small farming community had no schoolhouse, church, meeting hall, or elected officials, and the only town property was comprised of a "pound for unruly cows." In 1763, the town petitioned to be excused from paying province taxes, and, in 1700, asked the general court to dissolve their town charter. The acreage was divided up between the towns of Hollis, Milford, Brookline, and Amherst, New Hampshire.

Today, what remains of the town is limited, but spectacular to behold. Russ Dickerman, whose family once owned a great deal of the area, serves as Monson's caretaker and official tour guide. He has lovingly and carefully created and maintains a museum to the town in the Gould House, the only remaining home standing on the property. Filled with relics of the town, and many of his personal family heirlooms, he can be found in this museum or on the property most days. He loves to teach about the region's history and delights at entertaining new visitors with his tales.

Dickerman has also been open to teams of paranormal investigators exploring the area. Many, many visitors to the area believe that they have had encounters with the spirits of Monson's former residents, and Russ enjoys hearing about these experiences and sharing some of his own. Ghost Quest, the highly regarded paranormal investigation team lead by Demonologist and Occult Sciences expert Katie Boyd and the internationally acclaimed Psychic Medium Beckah Boyd, has declared the location to be certifiably haunted and a certificate indicating such can be viewed in the Gould House.

Above from left:
West Monson Road.

A marsh area off of West Monson Road.

A long, winding pathway through the woods at Monson Center.

Opposite:
The only communal property the town had, a "pound for unruly cows."

AUTHOR NOTES

We visited Monson Center on a bright summer day with the Boyds and were pleased to be able to meet Russ at the Gould House. He gave us a tour of the home and showed us a number of interesting Colonial Period artifacts. We picked up a map of the trail system that would take us through the center of the former settlement and we hit the woods.

Unlike some of the ghost towns in New England, the trek to the home sites was not especially arduous and the map was easy to read. Each cellar hole had an accompanying informational plaque that indicated who had lived in the home, their contributions to the community, and other interesting facts.

Russ, with support of the "Friends of Monson," has made the property accessible, educational, and perhaps most notably, quite beautiful. We enjoyed strolling the property, learning about this historic location and soaking in some summer sun in the gardens. We highly recommend stopping by the sight in the spring or summer when the beautiful trees and fields green up and the flower beds are in full bloom. It's a wonderful and serene location. Be sure to allow ample time to chat with Russ; he is the heart and soul of the Monson Center ghost town and it would be a very different place without him.

~*Summer*

VISITORS' INFORMATION

Though the ghost town is actually in Milford, New Hampshire, to get to it you must travel to Adams Road in the nearby town of Hollis. From Route 101, take Route 122 and follow it into Hollis. Take a right onto Hayden Road and travel for about a mile. Turn right onto Federal Hill Road and then onto Adams Road. There is a dirt parking area for a few cars and a sign that clearly labels the sight. After walking down the dirt pathway a short ways, the forest will open up to a large field and you will see the Gould House in the distance.

Opposite page: Clockwise from bottom left:

A cellar hole at the Monson Center Ghost Town.

Dr. Brown's home site is one of many scattered along the trails of Monson Center.

The Gould House, still flying the British Grand Union Flag.

This page:

Beautiful landscaping outside the Gould House.

Lovely landscaping and a still-functional water pump.

6
BUNKER HILL MONUMENT
Boston, Massachusetts

Now, at famous Bunker Hill,
Even though we lost, it was quite a thrill,
The rebel Colonel Prescott proved he was wise;
Outnumbered and low on ammunition
As the British stormed his position
He said, "Hold your fire till you see the whites of their eyes!"

~BOB DOROUGH
"THE SHOT HEARD ROUND THE WORLD"

On April 19, 1775, the American Revolutionary War began in Lexington and Concord, Massachusetts, and with the start of the fighting, the citizens of Boston probably suspected that they were going to be a big focus in the plans of the British Regulars. The city was held by British General Thomas Gage and nearly 5,000 soldiers. The key to holding Boston was control of the hills on the Charlestown Peninsula. From those vantage points one could see any approach from either the city or from Boston's Harbor. The American rebels learned that the British were going to occupy Charlestown, so they mobilized. When the British Regulars arrived, the Americans, lead by Colonel William Prescott, had managed to fortify Breed's Hill. General Gage ordered the hill to be captured. There were three assaults by the British between 3:30 p.m. and 5:30 p.m. The first skirmish occurred when the British landed near Charlestown. They were met by sniper fire from the American forces and the British retaliated by setting Charlestown on fire. The British attempted to flank the rebel forces but were hampered by clever obstacles and dedicated fighters. The first British assault was successfully turned back. The British forces immediately regrouped and began the second assault. It was a costly failure. The Americans were elated with their success; however, they were unskilled, undermanned, and lacking in supplies; the British weren't defeated. On the third assault, the British drove past the American's obstacles, only being held back long enough to cover Colonel Prescott's retreat. The surviving Americans retreated to Cambridge, only being pursued by the British to as far as the nearby Bunker Hill.

The British had won Breed's Hill, but it had been a hard-won battle and a hard-learned lesson. Out of 2,200 British Soldiers, 1,034 were casualties. In this one battle, they lost one quarter of the officers they would lose in the entire war. On the American side, there were 400 to 600 casualties out of 2,500 to 4,000 men. In these bloody two hours, much was learned on both sides. The British learned that this rabble of upstarts were a dedicated group of soldiers who were determined to stand up for themselves and their colony. The Americans learned the horror of war and the need for strong leadership, which was soon

The Bunker Hill Monument.

Major General Dr. Joseph Warren's statue in the Bunker Hill Exhibit Lodge.

provided when, on July 2, 1775, George Washington assumed the role of Commander-in-Chief of the Continental Army.

The first monument on Breed's Hill was built by the King Solomon's Lodge of Masons in 1794. It was an eighteen-foot wooden pillar with a gilt urn on the top, built in honor of Major General Dr. Joseph Warren. Dr. Warren had the chance to lead the American forces in the battle. He did have a higher rank than Colonel Prescott, but Dr. Warren refused command, knowing that Prescott had more experience with warfare than he did. Dr. Warren was killed in the final assault on the hill and there is a statue of him in the Bunker Hill exhibit lodge. In 1823, the Bunker Hill Monument Association purchased the land and started building the monument that stands today. On June 17, 1843, the monument was dedicated.

A 221-foot granite obelisk now stands at the summit of Breed's Hill and the more hearty visitors can climb the 294 steps to the top of the obelisk for no charge, although donations are appreciated. There is an exhibit lodge directly beside the monument and a statue of Colonel Prescott in front of the monument keeping watch over the Harbor.

The order to "hold your fire until you see the whites of their eyes" would have been so that the first rounds of fire were effective and coordinated. The idea was to always have some men firing while others were loading their guns. It is not known if this exact phrase was used, but the men were told to aim low and target the British Officers.

The Battle is known as the Battle of Bunker Hill because Colonel Prescott's orders were to fortify and defend that hill; however, when he arrived in the area, he chose Breed's Hill as his battleground.

A statue of Colonel Prescott stands in front of the massive 221-foot obelisk.

GOD'S LITTLE ACRE CEMETERY

Newport, Rhode Island

You lament not the dead, but lament the trouble of making a grave; the way of the ghost is longer than the grave.

~AFRICAN PROVERB

Newport, Rhode Island, home to the world-famous "Newport Mansions," was built on the backs of kidnapped West Africans. Hailing from the Gold, Ivory, Guinea, and Cape Coasts, several thousands of African servants served in the homes of rum distillers, seaport supervisors, and merchants. At the peak of the Colonial Period, roughly one in three families had a household servant, and slaves made up nearly one-third of the total population of Newport. The town played a large part of the Transatlantic Slave Trade. As society progressed and times changed, a great deal of these "servants," infrequently called "slaves," became "Free Africans" and chose to remain in the area, and, in 1780, the first Free African Benevolent Society was founded. These Free Africans were often regarded as more highly skilled and trained than their southern counterparts, and, in the 2005 documentary film *Stories From Stone: Africans in Colonial Rhode Island* by filmmaker Elizabeth Delude Dix, Newport Town Historian Keith Stokes noted that their skills "helped build and sustain early American commerce."

Remembering Their Own

Newport is also home to the historically significant cemetery known as "God's Little Acre," so named by the local Africans and African Americans. With stones dating back to the late 1600s, God's Little Acre has some of the oldest, and possibly largest, surviving collection of these tombstones. Once numbering about 300, the stones have not stood up well to the harsh New England winters, and the majority have fallen into a state of disrepair.

Pompe "Zingo" Stevens, the servant of local stonecutter John Stevens, is credited with carving the majority of the tombstones placed for his fellow Africans and is regarded as being the first true artist in early America. On perhaps the oldest stone of its kind in the yard, with a date of 1768, it is noted:

This stone was cut by Pompe Stevens in memory of his brother Cufrie Gibbs

Nestled underneath the trees at the rear of God's Little Acre, side by side, are the plots of Zingo's wives. Even in the 1700s, lifespans for women fell short of their male counterparts, and Zingo married and was predeceased by three wives: Philis, Elizabeth, and Violet. Their tombstones were, of course, all constructed by Zingo. If he is buried in the area, the tomb is unmarked, but it does seem likely if he had acquired the land to inter his three wives together, that there would have been sufficient space for his.

Author Notes

We had no difficulty finding the cemetery, but because the tombstones aren't fenced into a separate yard, it is difficult to spot the stone. Many visitors to the site, as well as the town of Newport and other educational resources, have photographed a large, ornate black sign with gold accents that introduces the tale of how the cemetery came to be. When we visited Newport over Memorial Day Weekend, we circled the cemetery, driving around and around the same city block, trying to locate the sign. Without the assurance the sign would have afforded us, we eventually parked our vehicle and searched out God's Little Acre by foot. Hopefully, the sign was down for repairs and will be returned shortly, but if you find yourself in a similar situation, we'd suggest you follow our strategy, and walk by foot through the grounds, keeping the street to your left side.

~Summer

Visitors' Information

God's Little Acre is located within the Common Burying Ground on Farewell Street in Newport, Rhode Island.

God's Little Acre Cemetery in Newport, Rhode Island.

Clockwise from right:

Hanging tree branches partially obscure a tombstone at God's Little Acre.

"Here lieth Moll, wife of Peter, servant to Robert Baker."

"In memory of Peggy, a late servant of Mrs. Peggy Searing."

Zingo Stevens, one of Newport's most well-known stone carvers, crafted this tombstone for his late wife, Elizabeth.

A lush purple Azaelia marks springtime at God's Little Acre.

27

HARDSCRABBLE AND SNOW TOWN RIOT MEMORIALS

Providence, Rhode Island

The challenge of social justice is to evoke a sense of community that we need to make our nation a better place, just as we make it a safer place.

~MARIAN WRIGHT EDELMAN

Despite founder Roger Williams's high ideals, Providence, Rhode Island, has had some rough times and the town has markers for two such incidents. In the span of ten years, Providence was the location of two race riots. Providence was still embracing Roger Williams's belief in freedom; this is evidenced by the fact that about thirty-seven years before the Civil War, at the time of the first riot, it was possible for a black man to vote in local elections (the right to vote being based solely on land ownership and there were several black men who qualified and did participate in local politics).

However, with the industrialization of the area, there were more lower income jobs that did not include housing. Farm work and "live-in domestic situations" were no longer being offered. This meant people needed affordable housing. What they found was cheap housing.

The area of Addison Hollow, also known as the Hardscrabble area, was a mostly black neighborhood, but along with the homes, there were bars, bordellos, and other "shady" businesses. The "respectable" residents of Providence were incensed by the wickedness that was flourishing in their city.

On October 18, 1924, a conflict escalated. A black man refusing to get off the sidewalk to allow white people through. Before this,

there was a newspaper article about roving gangs of black men forcing white pedestrians off sidewalks. Perhaps these unsubstantiated reports instigated the incident, or the story was twisted through time and is mistakenly reported as the spark that set this flame. Whatever the cause, that night, hundreds of white rioters swarmed through Hardscrabble tearing buildings down. Some accounts indicate that the rioters targeted "places of ill-repute." Others say the mob was indiscriminate in the destruction. Local law enforcement failed to contain the riot and approximately twenty homes of black citizens were destroyed. Only four people were tried for the rioting, and of those four, only one was found guilty. He received a light sentence.

The general public made it clear that they supported the rioters and were openly congratulatory to participants. It was thought of as a community service and focus was placed on the depravity of the area.

Almost seven years later, the area of Snow Town, possibly at the same location as Addison Hollow, suffered an attack. This time the riots began on September 21, 1831, when there was a dispute between white sailors and black residents. The conflict escalated and a black man came out of one of the homes and warned the sailors away. When that didn't work, he shot and killed one of the sailors. This lead to two more nights of riots and many homes were destroyed. However, times had changed since the 1824 riots, and instead of ineffectual local constables, the militia was called out. Unfortunately, the militia was vastly outnumbered by the mob (estimated 180 militia to over 1,000 rioters). The mob had no fear of the militiamen, since it was well remembered how, in 1824, the law just stood and watched without interfering. The mob taunted the militia, daring them to fire. The militia unable to contain the crowd and in danger of being disarmed, thus arming the mob, fired into the crowd. Four men were killed and the mob dispersed.

The aftermath of this riot was hugely different. While many citizens were not happy with the outcome, the overall sentiment was that law and order needed to prevail. It was made obvious that the citizens were supportive of the militia. The residents of Snow Town were viewed as victims (more so than the residents of Hardscrabble), but public sentiment was that the residents weren't completely innocent in sparking the rioting.

AUTHOR NOTES

The Hardscrabble and the Snow Town riot monuments are interesting in that the people of Providence have chosen to memorialize a piece of their darker history—whether for the African Americans who want to remember the hardships people of their race suffered and overcame, or the Whites who wish to acknowledge the wrongs of our past and remind all of us that there is hope. Things have gotten better and, someday, we will reach the point where race is no longer a basis of discrimination.

~Cathy

VISITORS' INFORMATION

You can find the Hardscrabble marker in the traffic island of the intersection of North Main Street and Canal Street; this is the probable location of Hardscrabble. The marker for the Snow Town riot is located at the Roger Williams National Memorial, not far from the Hardscrabble monument.

From top:
The site of the Hardscrabble Riot of 1824 in Providence, Rhode Island.

The plaque commemorating the Snow Town Riot of 1831 in Providence, Rhode Island.

9
AMISTAD MEMORIAL
New Haven, Connecticut

This man is black. We can all see that. But, can we also see as easily, that which is equally true? That he is the only true hero in this room. Now, if he were white, he wouldn't be standing before this court fighting for his life. If he were white and his enslavers were British, he wouldn't be standing, so heavy the weight of the medals and honors we would bestow upon him. Songs would be written about him. The great authors of our times would fill books about him. His story would be told and retold, in our classrooms. Our children, because we would make sure of it, would know his name as well as they know Patrick Henry's. Yet, if the South is right, what are we to do with that embarrassing, annoying document, The Declaration of Independence? What of its conceits? "All men created equal," "inalienable rights," "life, liberty," and so on and so forth? What on Earth are we to do with this? I have a modest suggestion. [Tears papers in half]"

~ANTHONY HOPKIN'S PORTRAYAL OF
JOHN QUINCY ADAMS
IN THE 1997 FILM *AMISTAD,* BY STEVEN SPEILBERG

In 1839, Spaniard Captain Jose Ruiz sailed the ship *La Amistad* from the Havana, Cuba coast and ultimately became a major symbol in a worldwide movement to abolish slavery. The ship was transporting a cargo of fifty-three African adults and four children, who had been previously kidnapped, illegally sold into slavery, and bound for the *Puerto Principe.* The ship was named for the Spanish word for "friendship," but the situation was anything but friendly when a 26 year old named Sengbe Peih, later known by the name Joseph Cinque in the United States, used a stolen file to lead a mutinous revolt against their captors and boarded the ship *Amistad.* The captain and ship's cooks were immediately killed, but the majority of the crew was allowed to live, so that the vessel could continue to sail. Pieh and the others had hoped to disembark at the next sight of land and find assistance in returning to their home. The ship's navigator, Don Pedro Montez, mislead the Africans and steered the *Amistad* towards the

Opposite:
The Amistad Memorial stands on the site of the jail where the Africans were held; the place is now New Haven, Connecticut City Hall.

shore of the United States. Lieutenant Thomas R. Godney and the USS *Washington* of the United States Revenue Cutter Service, overtook the vessel and commandeered control back from the Africans. With the ship under control, he delivered the slaves to the authorities in New Haven, Connecticut, rather than the closer cities in New York. His rationale for doing so was that slavery had been unequivocally abolished in New York State and the laws in Connecticut were more favorable to conviction of the mutineers because the slavery laws were much more lenient.

Supreme Court Trial

In 1841, the United States versus The Libellants and Claimants of the Schooner *Amistad* was tried before the U.S. Supreme Court. As John Quincy Adams pleaded for the release of the imprisoned Africans in the criminal trial, the world watched. It took Judge Smith Thompson only three days to rule because the *Amistad* was a Spanish ship and the mutiny had taken place in Spanish waters where the United States had no jurisdiction to assign any form of punishment. A civil proceeding was subsequently launched and the trial was widely publicized and garnered a considerable amount of attention the world over.

When all was said and done, it took Judge Andrew Judson less than a week to rule that the initial transport across the Atlantic had been illegal and a violation of the international abolishment of the slave trade. He indicated that the captives were not legally slaves, and were, therefore, free men; their illegal confinement meant that they were within their rights to take whatever measures necessary to secure their freedom, including the use of force. This finding was affirmed by the Supreme Court on March 9, 1841, and substantially aided in the advancement of the Abolitionist Movement. New Haven abolition supporters took the remaining thirty-six men and three girls who had been held during the trial to nearby Farmington, Connecticut, considered to be "The Grand Central Station of the Underground Railroad." Arrangements for return passage to Africa were made in 1842.

The *Amistad* Remembered

A replica of the *Amistad*, The Freedom Schooner *Amistad*, was created in 2000, and on its maiden voyage, sailed from the seaport in Mystic, Connecticut to New Haven. In addition to a 2010 sail to Cuba as part of the Caribbean Freedom Tour, it voyaged and docked for a two-month visit to the West African town of Sierra Leone in 2007-2008, the home of many of the captives. Owned and maintained by Amistad America Inc., the ship provides extensive educational programming about the incident and related themes of peace and tolerance. It is open to the public.

Additionally, a larger-than-life, 3D bronze memorial was placed on the site of the jail that held the Africans during the court trials, currently the site of the New Haven City Hall, and is part of the Connecticut Freedom Trail. This fourteen-foot-tall triangular work of art was designed by sculptor Ed Hamilton and was installed in 1992. Each bronze panel depicts to a phase of the *Amistad* incident, beginning with an image of Pieh and the others before the kidnapping, continuing to a portrayal of a court scene, and concluding with a representation of the Africans preparing to board a ship back home. Unable to be viewed from street level, and only from the second floor and above within the City Hall, is the top of the triangular piece. Projecting from the surface is the image of a drowning man, with a barely exposed face, hand, and other body parts, meant to evoke images of Africans who jumped or were thrown overboard during the journey.

VISITORS' INFORMATION

The Amistad Memorial can be viewed at 165 Church Street in front of the City Hall in New Haven, Connecticut. Metered parking spaces are available across the street from the memorial, along the edges of a park in which the Africans were brought daily to exercise.

"MAKE US FREE"

This monument is a memorial to the 1839 Amistad revolt and its leader, Singbe Pieh also known as Joseph Cinque. Singbe was one of the millions of Africans kidnapped from their home, transported in bondage to the Americas, sold into slavery in Cuba. Other men and four children were bound aboard the schooner. During a storm, Singbe Pieh successfully freed himself. Africans seized the ship, but their ordeal was far from over. For weeks at sea, they were captured off Long Island...

The Amistad Memorial in New Haven, Connecticut.

Sengbe Peih / Joseph Cinque is tried before the U.S. Supreme Court.

The Accusation Stone
Milford, New Hampshire

Epitaphs serve many purposes. They can provide insight into the person memorialized, the life they lived, or how they died. There is another type of epitaph, however; it is an accusation or revenge stone. These are usually designed by the family or friends left behind who feel their loved one's death was the result of others, especially if those others went unpunished.

One of the most verbose examples of this type of epitaph is the one that completely covers Caroline H. Cutter's stone in Milford, New Hampshire:

Caroline H.
Wife of Calvin Cutter, M.D.
Murdered by the Baptist ministry and Baptist Churches as follows:
September 28, 1838, age 33.
She was accused of lying in a Church meeting by the Rev. D.D. Pratt and Deacon Albert-Adams
Was condemned by the church unheard.
She was reduced to poverty by Deacon William Wallace.
When an expert council was asked of the Milford Baptist Church, by The advice of their committee, George Raymond, Calvin Averill and Andrew Hutchinson,
They voted not to receive any communication upon the subject:
The Rev. Mark Carpenter said he thought as the good old Deacon Pearson said, "We have got Cutter down and it is best to keep him down."
The intentional and malicious destruction of her character and happiness, As above described, destroyed her life. Her last words upon the subject were,
"Tell the truth and the iniquity will come out."

The story behind this stone revolves around Caroline's husband. Dr. Calvin Cutter was the underwriter for the building of a new Baptist Church. The minister embezzled the money, leaving Dr. Cutter to deal with the consequences. When Cutter went to the church council and the pastor, he was refused a public hearing. Dr. and Mrs. Cutter were accused of lying and were kicked out of the congregation. The stress and shame of being treated so badly was more than Caroline could stand and her health failed; she died soon after.

Dr. Cutter presented a resolution to the citizens of Nashua and Nashville, New Hampshire:

The charges against the Baptist Church and Society are cheating, lying, keeping false church records, condemning persons unheard, destroying the character and life of Caroline H. Cutter.

The resolution was passed unanimously by the gathering. Soon after this meeting, Dr. Cutter gave up his medical practice and traveled as a lecturer. During the American Civil War, he served as a medical doctor for the Union troops.

The "Accusation Stone" in Milford, New Hampshire.

Carrie Cutter's stone.

AUTHOR NOTES

The stone of Caroline is particularly interesting in that Dr. Cutter so wanted to air his grievances that not only is the stone crammed from top to bottom with this story, but neither her date of birth nor death are listed.

It is also worth noting that another stone has been placed directly in front of Caroline's stone. About one foot separates Caroline's stone from a memorial for Carrie Cutter, Calvin and Caroline's daughter. Carrie Cutter died assisting her father during the Civil War as a nurse. She was the first woman to enter into the service of her country in the Civil War and the first woman to die at her post during the war. With such an impressive resume, she is on the "Roll of Honor" in the Congressional Library and was buried with Military Honors due a Colonel.

While the memorial is a very nice testament to Carrie, one has to wonder, though, with the placement of this stone, was this is an attempt to literally cover up the Accusation Stone or was this second stone an honest attempt to honor a war veteran and make amends for the Cutter family's sacrifices?

~*Cathy*

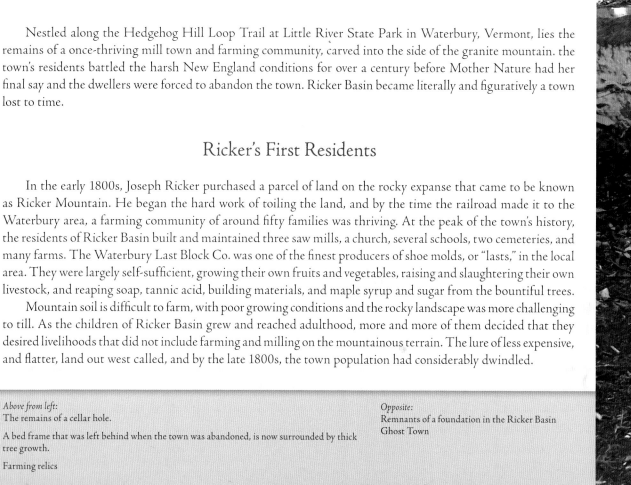

11
RICKER BASIN GHOST TOWN
Waterbury, Vermont

Nestled along the Hedgehog Hill Loop Trail at Little River State Park in Waterbury, Vermont, lies the remains of a once-thriving mill town and farming community, carved into the side of the granite mountain. the town's residents battled the harsh New England conditions for over a century before Mother Nature had her final say and the dwellers were forced to abandon the town. Ricker Basin became literally and figuratively a town lost to time.

Ricker's First Residents

In the early 1800s, Joseph Ricker purchased a parcel of land on the rocky expanse that came to be known as Ricker Mountain. He began the hard work of toiling the land, and by the time the railroad made it to the Waterbury area, a farming community of around fifty families was thriving. At the peak of the town's history, the residents of Ricker Basin built and maintained three saw mills, a church, several schools, two cemeteries, and many farms. The Waterbury Last Block Co. was one of the finest producers of shoe molds, or "lasts," in the local area. They were largely self-sufficient, growing their own fruits and vegetables, raising and slaughtering their own livestock, and reaping soap, tannic acid, building materials, and maple syrup and sugar from the bountiful trees.

Mountain soil is difficult to farm, with poor growing conditions and the rocky landscape was more challenging to till. As the children of Ricker Basin grew and reached adulthood, more and more of them decided that they desired livelihoods that did not include farming and milling on the mountainous terrain. The lure of less expensive, and flatter, land out west called, and by the late 1800s, the town population had considerably dwindled.

36

Above from left:
The remains of a cellar hole.

A bed frame that was left behind when the town was abandoned, is now surrounded by thick tree growth.

Farming relics

Opposite:
Remnants of a foundation in the Ricker Basin Ghost Town

Washed Away

On November 3rd and 4th, 1927, torrential rains caused immense flooding. The remaining farmers were cut off from the community members who had moved to the Winnoski Valley, where the citizens had to be rescued from their rooftops. When the water had receded, 55 people were dead and property damaged exceeded 13.5 million dollars. After a second flood in 1934, the U.S. Army Corps of Engineers and the Civilian Conservation Corps built the Waterbury Dam and, later, a power plant.

The last resident of Ricker Basin was Peter Tatro. He resided at the farm and sugar house, built by Joseph Ricker in 1816, which had been constantly farmed for over ninety years. Town lore suggests that Tatro burned the property to the ground in a land ownership dispute.

Stones and Bones of the Basin

Just up the road from the Ricker Sugar House lies a small, thirty feet by thirty feet, family cemetery consisting of fifteen plots. Unlike the maple and birch trees that are indigenous to the area, the cemetery walls are circled by white cedars that were planted by the Rickers to honor their loved ones. These Arbor Vitae's, or trees of life, were meant to give life to the deceased.

One unique aspect of the cemetery is the direction in which the stones are inscribed. Though the pale stone initially appears to be unmarked, when you enter the grounds, you will discover that the stones are marked on the side facing away from the path. It is unknown what inspired the Rickers to place the stones this way, but it does present a peaceful air to the spot.

With the exception of a few children who passed at birth or shortly thereafter, the majority of the Ricker family lived to be between 70 to 100 years of age. The first burial in the graveyard is that of Mary Ricker, who died in 1846 at the age of 78. The final burial took place when Florence Ricker died 75 years to the date of her birth.

The Hedgehog Hill Loop Trail is easily located from the Dalley Loop Trail. The hike to the cemetery is roughly two miles long and the Little River State Park has labeled it as a "moderate" hike. The trail is a steep incline, so be sure to wear appropriate footwear and bring

Clockwise from above:
Old farm roads twist throughout Ricker Basin

The reservoir created by the Waterbury Dam.

Remnants from Ricker's sugar house and other household items that remain on the original properties.

Rusty pieces of equipment provide reminders of the farming community that once flourished here.

Once useful, now cast off.

plenty of water. Take a moment to reflect on how difficult it would be to maneuver the ploughs, wagons, and timber down this steep grade. It does make it much more understandable why the flatter land in the west was so appealing to the younger generations.

Haunted Hikes

If you're up for an adventure, you may wish to join the state park rangers in a "Haunted History Hike" of the town. Along with a guided tour of the town's remains, you can visit the Ricker Cemetery as well as tour the only remaining building, the Goodell home. This property is said to contain an angry and vengeful spirit who is upset about the loss of his land. Whether you arrive for a day hike, a late night ghost hunt, or a weekend at any of the campsites, or lean-to's and cabins the park offers, enjoy the history and you just may catch sight of a real ghost in a New England ghost town.

AUTHOR NOTE

This Ghost Town is truly an amazing site, but as with most things in life, there is a price to pay for it! To make it to the remains of this lost town, you must hike a rather arduous, two-mile trail nearly straight up the side of a mountain. We made the error of choosing a hot and muggy July day to undertake this hike, and I can honestly say that it made a difference in how much we were able to enjoy the experience. We simply had not prepared for the type of hike we were to undertake. It's certainly a beautiful site, full of rich history, and we highly recommend you make time to visit when you are in the area; just be sure to wear proper shoes and be sure to stay hydrated!

~Summer

VISITORS' INFORMATION

The ghost town of Ricker Basin is located within Little Rivers State Park at 3444 Little River Road in Waterbury, Vermont. The homestead remains and cemetery can be found along the Hedgehog Hill Loop trail. It's a hike, but certainly worth the effort.

Clockwise from left:
The "Trees of Life," not indigenous to this area of Vermont, were planted by the residents of Ricker Basin to honor the deceased.

The cemetery in the Ricker Basin ghost town.

The tombstone of Mary Ricker, the first to be buried in the Ricker cemetery in 1846.

12

GREEN MOUNT CEMETERY
Montpelier, Vermont

Green Mount Cemetery is located at 251 State Street in Montpelier, Vermont. There are many beautiful stones and statues on this thirty-five-acre lot. They even have a Woodland Garden where people can be buried next to a small hiking trail along the back of the property. The cemetery was established in 1854 when Calvin Keith, a Montpelier lawyer, donated $1000 to the town toward the purchase price of $2,210 for the area.

When you first enter Green Mount Cemetery, you see an impressive structure. This is the Chapel, and you must drive through it to enter. This structure was donated by John E. Hubbard, whose monument is discussed further along, and was dedicated on June 12, 1905. It is a Gothic-style building that has seating for 60 to 100 people in the chapel for funeral services, and there is room for 62 bodies in a receiving vault. Sadly, the chapel has fallen into disuse. It does make for an awe-inspiring threshold for the equally impressive art that lies within the cemetery.

For the Sake of Atonement

John Erastus Hubbard was a source of considerable controversy in Montpelier that began when Fanny Hubbard-Kellogg died in 1890, only three months after her husband, Martin. The couple were originally from Montpelier and decided that, since they had no children, they would bequeath their fortune, more than $300,000, to the town of Montpelier. They wanted to set up a library in the town and build a chapel/gateway for Green Mount Cemetery. However, Fanny's nephew, John, had expected to receive a sizable inheritance from the couple. When he learned that he was to get none of the money, he contested the will. In a New York court, for that is where the couple was living when they died, the court overturned the will, and awarded the money to John Hubbard. Obviously, the people of Montpelier,

Above:
The Chapel/Vault at Green Mount Cemetery.

Opposite:
The gravesite of John Hubbard.

JOHN E. HUBBARD

where John also lived, were not happy to lose this huge sum of money. So the town officials went to the Supreme Court of Vermont. They hoped to force John into using the money as it had been stipulated in Martin and Fanny Hubbard-Kellogg's will. Instead, the issue was settled out of court. John agreed to provide $30,000 for the building of a library. In an attempt to placate the townfolk, Hubbard gave $60,000 to build and maintain the Kellogg-Hubbard Library. This deal, however, was not enough to appease some of the citizens of Montpelier. Hubbard's main detractor was John Burgess, a summer resident of Montpelier and friend of Martin Kellogg. Burgess made it his mission to obstruct any of Hubbard's plans. He wanted to punish Hubbard and the town officials who agreed to settle over the Kellogg's bequest. Burgess went so far as to turn a private library at the local YMCA into a rival library. He courted supporters and vilified anyone associated with the Kellogg-Hubbard Library.

The fighting continued until July 17, 1899, when John Hubbard died at the age of 51. The cause of death was cancer of the liver, but many felt that the strain of the battle with Burgess contributed to his early death. Hubbard's will may have led to the softening of the malice that was directed towards him. He left most of his money to the town, with $125,000 going to the library, $25,000 for the chapel gate at Green Mount Cemetery (see prior), about 100 acres of land to be used as a public park, $50,000 to maintain the park land, and $10,000 for the erection of his monument at Green Mount Cemetery. Almost exactly what the Kellogg estate had left to the town.

As for his monument, there is no documentation that Hubbard specified what he wanted for his memorial. It is likely that the executors of his will, former Vermont Governor William Dillingham and Kellogg-Hubbard trustee Arthur Farwell, requested something to help restore Hubbard's reputation. They turned to sculptor Karl Bitter, an emigre from Vienna, to create a fitting tribute.

Bitter had embraced a more secular approach to cemetery art, and he chose Thanatos, the Greek daemon personification, as the subject. "Thanatos" is a five-foot-high, bronze statue of a seated man, his head is thrown back and to the left, leaving his long neckline exposed. His lips are slightly parted, and his eyes are closed. He is draped in a winding sheet that is wrapped around his body.

The "Thanatos" sculpture is seated on an architectural piecee designed by another Austrian, Hans Kestranek. There is a flat granite stone behind the "Thanatos" sculpture and a stone slab at his feet. On either side of the statue are stone wreaths framing the monument's inscriptions.

To the right of the figure reads lines from William Cullen Bryant's poem "Thanatopsis."

> THOU GO NOT LIKE THE
> QUARRY SLAVE AT NIGHT
> SCOURGED TO HIS DUNGEON
> BUT SUSTAINED AND SOOTHED
> BY AN UNFALTERING TRUST

and to the left:

> APPROACH THY GRAVE
> LIKE ONE WHO WRAPS
> THE DRAPERY OF HIS COUCH
> ABOUT HIM AND LIES DOWN
> TO PLEASANT DREAM.

Bryant is not credited on the memorial, since he was so famous, it was believed everyone would recognize his work.

The memorial has also wormed its way into urban legend. It is said that if you sit in the lap of "Black Agnes," an odd nickname the statue has acquired, you will die within the next few weeks. There are tales of people drowning in the Winooski River just across the street from the cemetery, dying in car accidents, or expiring in any number of horrifying ways. We have been unable to find any verified deaths linked to the statue or the gravesite, but because the curse can take years to strike, it would be a hard thing to verify. Perhaps the site is truly cursed or maybe the story is just a continuation of the bad feelings people had against Hubbard in his life.

"Little Margaret"

If you turn left after entering the cemetery and follow the road, always veering right, you will come across the memorial for Margaret Pitkin. This incredibly detailed statue is located down a small hill in the north-western section of the grounds. "Little Margaret," as she is known locally, died of spinal meningitis on December 4, 1899, at the approximate age of six. The story goes that her grief-stricken parents, Carroll Perley Pitkin and Mary Devine Pitkin, provided a photograph to the sculptor and requested an exact replica be made. When the sculptor finished the monument, Margaret's father refused to pay for it, since the statue's boot was missing a button. However, when the sculptor showed the photograph he used to the little girl's father, she was, in fact, missing a button on her boot. Upon seeing this, the father paid in full. No one knows for sure who the sculptor was, but it is commonly believed that Harry Bertoli carved the likeness of Little Margaret. Bertoli was an Italian sculptor who had worked in Barre, Vermont, for many years before heading out to Montpelier. Experts say there are similarities between this statue and other memorials he is known to have carved. The detailing on this statue is breathtaking. Every element is carved precisely and lovingly detailed. A person could look at the monument for hours and still find a nuance that he or she may have missed. There are eyelets on her dress that look so delicate, you'd think it was real lace, and she wears a small medal. You can see a ring on her right hand and a string of pearls around her neck. There is also fine detail in the fence she is leaning against and the flowers. The statue and Margaret's short life inspired a song, written in 1985 by Dan Lidner. A few lines:

Fresh fallen snow on the newly dug grave of the girl with the sunlight in her smile...
Gathered around, all the many who loved her, whose lives she brightened for a while,
All the laughter and love in her seven short years were much more than some folks ever see,
Fare thee well, Margaret, you rest here in peace, while we cherish your sweet memory.

This statue is a complete must see.

AUTHOR NOTES

The artwork in this cemetery is incredibly beautiful and is something any lover of sculpture should make time for, if in the area. On the topic of the "Black Agnes" legend, there are many variations to the tale. Some stories claim you must sit on the statue at midnight, others have no time indicated, and there is even a version where you must kiss the statue. The consequences also vary from story to story. In most, you will die in a specified amount of time. Others say you will be cursed with bad luck, and, my favorite, "something will happen to you."

As I am prone to do when faced with these types of legends, I took the challenge, visited this site, and sat on Thanatos' lap. At the time of writing, I am still alive – although I've had two computers die and three broken teeth in this time period. So, there's either a bad luck curse or there is the fact that I've been using old computers and I am, admittedly, rather clumsy. Also I now have two potential death curses following me. I have sat on the lap of Thanatos/Black Agnes, and I've sat on the cursed "throne" at The Little People's Village in Middlebury, Connecticut, about a year ago. So, perhaps, the next cursed spot we hit, I'll let my co-author take a seat.

~Cathy

The statue of six year old Margaret Pitkin.

13

SLEEPY HOLLOW CEMETERY

Concord, Massachusetts

The Sleepy Hollow Cemetery, off Bedford Street in Concord, Massachusetts, was designed by the landscape architects Cleveland and Copeland in 1855. The cemetery was dedicated on September 29, 1855, by Ralph Waldo Emerson, who was later buried at the site. It is particularly fitting that Emerson spoke at the dedication, since it was his writing and beliefs that inspired the aesthetic principles of the site. Emerson was a leader of the Transcendentalist Movement. His essay "Nature," published anonymously in 1836, was the catalyst for the movement to become a major philosophical movement in the United States.

The concept of transcendentalism can be a bit vague. Most descriptions discuss those who were part of the movement, and readers are suppose to infer the meaning from authors' known writings and actions. One of the best descriptions is that Transcendentalism calls upon people to view objects in the world as small versions of the whole universe and to trust their personal intuitions. It was a rethinking of not only the world around them, but of how a person should interact with the world around them. The authors were closely tied to the abolitionist movement and were interested in finding a balance between science and spirituality.

Many notables are buried at Sleepy Hollow. There is even a section named "Author's Ridge." Here, on a small hillside at the back of the cemetery, you can see Cat's Pond, if you peek through the copious trees. Louisa May Alcott, author of *Little Women*, is buried here with her family, and you will also find the graves of Nathaniel and Sophia Hawthorne. Nathaniel wrote such books as *The Scarlet Letter* and *The House of Seven Gables* and Sophia was a noted painter. Harriet M. Lothrop, who wrote *The Five Little Peppers* as Margaret Sydney, is also buried on the hillside. Ralph Waldo Emerson, too, is here, buried with his family.

There is a small marker tucked away on the path leading up Author's Ridge. As you go up the path, on the left-hand side is The Echo Tree. When playing "Taps," there is one musician playing the piece in front of the crowd, while a second musician is hidden from the crowd playing the echo. This marker identifies the spot where the echo trumpeter is hidden away. In 2006, two Concord-Carlisle High School band's trumpeters requested that the city mark the spot where so many high school musicians have stood just to get that perfect echo.

Daniel Chester French, sculptor and designer of the Melvin Memorial and the statue of Abraham Lincoln at the Lincoln Memorial in Washington, D.C., is buried on Chestnut Path in the cemetery. His location isn't far from Author's Ridge and is just a short distance from the Melvin Memorial (discussed in Chapter 24).

Above:
Notable burials and spots in the Sleepy Hollow Cemetery; (from the left) the Thoreaus, Henry Wadsworth Longfellow, The Echo Tree , Louisa Alcott, the Hawthornes, the Emmersons, Harriet M. Lothrop aka Margaret Sydney, and Samuel French.

AUTHOR NOTES

This is a great stop for anyone who is a fan of history, writing, or art, and the landscaping here is a piece of art itself. It has the feel of a woodland walk. There are trees, flowers, and greenery everywhere, and while everything has been, obviously, well planned out, it does not feel contrived. It feels like something that has grown organically.

~*Cathy*

VISITORS' INFORMATION

Sleepy Hollow Cemetery is prominently located on Bedford Street in Concord, Massachusetts. Take the Prichard Gate and follow Upland Avenue to the rear of the cemetery, where you will find a small parking area near Author's Ridge. Also near Prichard Gate is the Melvin Memorial along Union Avenue. For more information on the Melvin Memorial, see Chapter 24.

Right from top:
The beautiful Sleepy Hollow Cemetery in springtime.

Author's Ridge at Sleep Hollow Cemetery in Concord, Massachusetts.

14

THE NATIONAL MONUMENT TO THE FOREFATHERS

Plymouth, Massachusetts

The largest granite monument in the entire U.S. has stood stoically for over 100 years on a small hill overlooking "America's Hometown," Plymouth, Massachusetts. A tribute to the lives and lessons of the *Mayflower* Pilgrims, it reaches an impressive eighty-one feet high and faces Plymouth Harbor, with an approximation of the direction across the sea towards Plymouth, England. A pilgrimage site for followers of the Christian faith in America, its size and stature alone make it a notable and remarkable, even by New England memorial standards.

Design and Erection

Commissioned by the Pilgrim Society, this awe-inspiring work of art was conceived by Boston architect, illustrator, and sculptor Hammatt Billings. His original draft of the design specified a height of 150 feet, which was merely one foot shy of the Statue of Liberty, from base to torch. When funding became short during the war, his design was scaled back considerably, though it did not diminish the artistic merit of the piece. Rising from a 45-foot-high octagonal pedestal base containing four small faces, four large faces, and the names of the *Mayflower* Pilgrims, is the form of a woman called "Faith." On four diagonal buttresses jutting out from the small faces,

15-foot-tall allegorical figures perch that personify ideals held by the Forefathers

The Pilgrim Society, with assistance from the Grand Lodge of Masons of Massachusetts, laid the cornerstone for the monument in 1859. The tribute was completed in October of 1888 and dedicated in August of 1889 "erected by a grateful people in remembrance of their labors, sacrifices, and sufferings for the cause of civil and religious liberty." The monument was added to the National Register of Historic Places in 1974 for "possessing significant value in commemorating and illustrating the history of the United States" and the site was maintained by the Pilgrim Society through 2001, when it sold the land and monument to the Commonwealth of Massachusetts.

Symbolism Rich

The National Monument to our Forefathers is meant to be "read" from the top to the bottom. Starting at the top, and arguably the most impressive feature of the Monument, is the 6-foot-tall statue of "Faith." This 180-ton statue shows a classically draped woman who stands with one foot perched upon a representation of Plymouth Rock. She was intended to be the personification of faith and symbolize the core virtue that inspired the Pilgrims' journey to the New World. She holds an open Bible in her

The National Monument to the Forefathers in Plymouth, Massachusetts, the largest granite memorial in the United States.

The personification of Faith.

left hand with her right index finger pointed heavenwards. Continuing to "read" down the monument, perched below Faith, are the core doctrine and values of "Liberty," "Law," "Education," and "Morality."

Liberty

Liberty is embodied by a helmeted male draped in the skin of a lion. He cradles a sword in his right arm and holds a broken chain in his left hand. Billings intended to communicate the notion that peace rests under the protection of liberty and as a reminder that tyranny can always be trumped and overthrown by liberty.

The high reliefs to either side of Liberty include a portrayal of a woman holding a horn overflowing with food and drink, demonstrating a flourishing time of peace, and a king laid low to represent the power of liberty in the overthrowing of tyrannical forces.

Law

The importance of the creation and maintenance of laws, Law is displayed as a seated, cloth-draped male holding a large book or tome. What has become a highly recognizable personification of Justice, a woman holding a sword and a set of scales, supports Law's seat.

The companion high relief depicts Mercy.

Education

Wisdom and Youth, lead by the experience of elders, surround the personification of Education. This draped woman, pointing to a book in her lap, encourages a legacy of lifelong learning and the acquisition of new skills with which to support the community as a whole.

Morality

Arguably the highest doctrine instilled by our Forefathers is that of Morality in all areas of one's life. Holding "God's Book," a tablet commonly interpreted as containing The Ten Commandments, and

the scroll of Revelations in her right hand, a robed woman sits serenely before Faith with eyes cast towards the horizon. The Prophet Moses is depicted presenting the tablets of Law and an Evangelist writing in a book would have exemplified the Pilgrims' sense of Morality.

Child Actor Controversy

The 2012 film *Monumental: In Search of America's National Treasure,* starring former child actor Kirk Cameron, heavily featured the monument. Cameron believes that the monument is "the most important one in the United States" and that if society resolved to follow the teachings and principles of the forefathers that the American society would see a dramatic change for the better. He goes as far as describing the monument as a "road map" that our ancestors predicted that we would one day need. The film did not meet with any acclaimed success and is largely unknown outside of the Christian community. It has not yet been reviewed by non-secular film critics.

AUTHOR NOTES

Regardless of your faith system, or lack thereof, or whether you see the great sculpture as a blueprint left behind by the Pilgrims, the monument is a must-see work of art. The sheer magnitude of its scope and size and the detailed depictions of life in the New World are truly worth a visit.

~Summer

VISITORS' INFORMATION

To visit the monument, follow Route 44 where it intersects with Route 3A/Court Street. Continue north on Allerton Street for about a block. It is walkable from the waterfront, Plymouth Rock, and Pilgrim Hall, if weather permits and you are able. Should you chose to drive, there is plenty of free parking at the monument site and it is handicap accessible.

WISDOM

TYRANNY

MORALITY

MERCY

Clockwise from top left:
Flanked by Education and Liberty statues, is a
list of the *Mayflower* passengers.

Law.

Morality with a depiction of the Pilgrims
arriving at Plymouth Rock.

Education.

15

THE UNKNOWN CONFEDERATE

Gray, Maine

The Civil War took the lives and futures of many of the nation's young men. Perhaps nowhere was this felt more deeply than in the small town of Gray, Maine. A third of their citizens over the age of 18 were sent to fight in "The War Between The States," and, proportionally, the town lost more of their sons to the war than any other town in Maine. The town cemetery serves as a final resting place to 179 Civil War soldiers, and every Memorial Day, the locals decorate their graves with "Old Glory," and on one, the Confederate flag.

Casualties of War

Amos and Sarah Colley were just one of the Gray families to have lost their son. Lieutenant Charles H. Colley, of the 10th Maine Volunteers, Company B, was one of the 8,000 Union soldiers who attacked a group of 20,000 Confederate troops at the Battle of Cedar Mountain, part of the Shenandoah Valley Campaign, on August 9, 1862. Of the 3,000 men killed or wounded in the intense fighting, Lt. Colley was one. Though quickly rushed to the hospital in Alexandria, Virginia, he passed away from his injuries on September 20, 1862. The Colleys received a telegram and learned of their son's passing, which was in and of itself a luxury many families were denied. Sarah begged her husband to pay the fee that the government charged to embalm and transport "Charlie" home. They began to plan for his burial and when the plain pine box arrived, it was placed in the living room of the family farmhouse. As friends and family stopped to pay their respects, the coffin remained closed, as was the custom, especially in light of the damaged condition that many of the bodies suffered. The box was due to remain closed, and, had it been, Amos and Sarah would have been spared the shock of a lifetime. Just as the family was about to leave for the cemetery, Sarah asked that the coffin be pried open so that she might see her beloved Charlie one last time. As the lid was removed, however, she discovered that it was not her son, and that a grave mistake had been made. There, in his place, lay the fully uniformed body of a "Johnny Reb," an unknown Confederate soldier.

How he had come to be delivered to the town was unclear, though the incidence was reportedly not all that uncommon during the war. Historians believe that the most likely causes of the mix ups were due to both the young men fighting at Cedar Mountain, passing away closely together in the Alexandria hospital, or being of similar name. An equally likely theory was that a simple clerical error had placed "Gray," referring to his uniform color and role as a Confederate, in the spot where his hometown should have been.

Regardless of the error that occurred, one fact was clear to Sarah Amos. Though the deceased young man was not her son, he was certainly someone's son, and as the government did not have the provisions to return him to Virginia, she felt an obligation to see him properly buried. In the plot intended for Charlie now lays the Stranger. When the Lieutenant's body arrived a week later, he was buried in the cemetery in a plot just 100 feet away.

A Stone to Match the Others

The "Ladies of Gray," a group of mothers whose sons had been killed, wounded, or were missing in the Civil War, raised funds from within the community to erect a stone for the Unknown Confederate. Of similar size, color, and style of engraving to his Union counterparts in the cemetery, the following stone was inscribed:

> Stranger
> – A soldier of the late war –
> died 1862
> Erected by the Ladies of Gray

Each year the gravesite is brightened by as many geraniums as the "Boys In Blue" gravesites, and the colors of both the North and the South are flown.

AUTHOR NOTES

We visited the cemetery on an overcast afternoon in late winter. Despite being within sight of the Maine Turnpike, it's a peaceful enough spot. There are many beautiful stones, both old and new, and it is easy to spend an afternoon looking at them all. One of the most strikingly stunning obelisks we've ever seen sits near the Stranger's plot. With a Robin's Egg blue marbling that mirrors the sky at times, it is a truly unique stone and not to be forgotten.

~Summer

VISITORS' INFORMATION

The cemetery is located directly across the road from the Gray-New Gloucester (exit 63) on the Maine Turnpike. When you enter the cemetery, navigate to the furthermost path that runs along the edge of the grounds. This lane is within view of the Dunkin Donut's parking lot and is bordered by a metal fence. You will quickly come to a small metal signpost with a scroll on top, from which hangs a simple sign bearing the word "Stranger," with a small arrow. Travel by foot down this aisle and you will find the plot to the left and, about 100 feet southwesterly, the tomb of Lt. Colley.

Right from top:
A simple sign points the way to the Stranger.

The final resting place of The Unknown Confederate in Gray, Maine.

53

16
TOGUS NATIONAL CEMETERY
Augusta, Maine

They are dead; but they live in each Patriot's breast,
And their names are engraven on honor's bright crest.

~HENRY WADSWORTH LONGFELLOW

There is more to the Togus Complex in Augusta, Maine than just the Togus National Cemetery. In its history it has included everything from veterans' housing, care to a zoo, and all manner of entertainment. However, in the beginning, Togus National Cemetery was built upon the site of a broken dream.

The land had belonged to Horace Beals of Rockland, Maine, who intended the "Togus natural hot Springs" to be a resort or retreat for the wealthy. He built everything from horse stables, to a hotel, and even included a bowling alley and a racetrack. He envisioned a site that would be a rival for Saratoga Springs in New York, a popular hot springs resort. Unfortunately for Mr. Beals, his timing was terrible. Togus Springs opened in 1859, just as the nation was building up to the Civil War. It seems with war coming, few were interested in traveling to the new resort. Togus Springs became known locally as "Beals' Folly" and it was closed in 1863. Soon after, Mr. Beals died and the government obtained the property for $50,000. Not a bad price, considering Beals had spent over $250,000 on attractions.

In 1865, Abraham Lincoln signed an act to establish the National Asylum for Disabled Volunteer Soldiers to provide care for soldiers who had been disabled while serving in the Union forces during the Civil War. Togus admitted their first veteran on November 10, 1866. The facility grew until it was able to house about 3,000 veterans and even had it's own, somewhat limited, hospital.

Above:
Togus National Cemetery, Augusta, Maine.

Opposite:
"Old Glory" and small white stones in carefully placed rows.

Part of the early appeal for the site, besides the very low purchase price, was the relative isolation of the area. However, in 1890, a railroad and an electric trolley were built to bring people from the nearby city of Augusta and people traveling up the Kennebec River could now easily access the site with this new transportation. Togus National Cemetery became a popular spot for Sunday picnics. A zoo was built, as well as a hotel, theater, and bandstand. Forty years after Harold Beals built his resort, Togus had finally become the vacation spot he had imagined.

In July 1930, all agencies administering benefits to veterans in the United States were consolidated under the Veteran's Administration. To this day, there are still offices on the grounds and the Medical Center still offers care for Veterans. Then there is the cemetery or, actually, *cemeteries*.

The cemetery grounds are comprised of thirty-one acres and divided into two cemeteries. The West Cemetery was established in 1865, when the facilities were being built. It was closed for interments in 1936, when the East Cemetery was established. In 1961, the East Cemetery was also closed for interments – although on the V.A.'s website it does state that spaces occasionally become available, either due to a cancelled reservation or a disinterment. If either happens, the gravesite is made available to another eligible veteran. According to the website, such openings are handled on a "first-come, first-served basis."

AUTHOR NOTES

We visited Togus National Cemetery on an overcast April afternoon. Now I think that military cemeteries have a different feel than civilian sites. All the stones are uniform and well maintained. Everything is placed with...well, military precision. There are also strict rules about what can be left at the site. It does not feel antiseptic or cold here, though. The grounds are surrounded by trees and there is a hiking trail, part of the Capital Walks Trails. On the whole, the place seems to radiate a quiet dignity and gives a peaceful impression, just what I imagine old soldiers and their families would crave. It is a truly beautiful spot.

~Cathy

The name *"Togus"* comes from the Native American name *Worromontogus*, which means "mineral water."

Right:
A Celtic cross, beautiful in its simplicity, inscribed: "Let them rest in peace."

17
The Fitz Lane Memorial
Gloucester, Massachusetts

An artist is always alone: if he is an artist. No, what the artist needs is loneliness.

~Henry Miller

We found this memorial by a "happy accident." We were looking for the Fishermen's Wives Memorial in Gloucester, Massachusetts and headed in the exact opposite direction from where we needed to go. However, while we were turning around on the Harbor Loop, we spotted a statue on the hill. A combination of curiosity and a need to get out of the car for a bit led us up the knoll to this statue. What we found was a likeness of a wild-eyed man leaning into the wind, as his coat flapped behind him and it even appeared as though his hat had been bent by the wind. The artist focused on his subject by producing a pair of crutches tucked under his legs. He is the personification of artistic focus.

The statue was compelling and we searched for information on artist, subject, and sculptor – and is proof that a wrong turn isn't always a bad thing. Fitz H. Lane, the subject, was born in Gloucester, Massachusetts on December 19, 1804. Sadly, at the age of 18 months, Fitz was partially paralyzed. The cause is not known for certain, but some report that he ingested Jimsonweed, a poisonous weed that grew in the area. Other reports indicated he had polio. Whatever the reason for his paralysis, it formed his life.

Lane was the son of a sailmaker and grew up on or near the docks of Gloucester's busy waterfront. He was likely to become either a sailmaker, like his father, or take up a seafaring career. Instead, Fitz became one of America's most famous painters of marine subjects. His work fell out of favor, or style, soon after his death, in 1865, but has experienced a resurgence in popularity since the 1930s. Lane was not only a popular painter, but he was also

Opposite:
The Fitz Lane Memorial in Gloucester, Massachusetts.

a social reformer. Part of the American Temperance Movement and a Transcendentalist, he was also a part of the Spiritualist movement. Lane was a local boy who made it big, a good subject for a local art installation.

The story continues in the late 1960s when sculptor Alfred M. Duca moved to Gloucester. Duca was a well-established artist and innovator credited with creating polymer tempura paints, which allowed "overpainting," a difficult process for artists. He also developed the Styrofoam Vaporization Process, a metal casting method. Despite his dedication to his craft, he had another calling and began working with "troubled" and at-risk teenagers. In 1971, he convinced the town of Gloucester and its community members to help fund a restoration project of an old town cemetery. While people were at first hesitant, and more than a little distrustful of these long-haired delinquents in their neighborhood, the work was done, and done well. People were beginning to be more supportive. The Gloucester Experiment, as it was called by the kids, grew from one project to another. The success of the program spread and, with the help of the Prudential Company, the Channel One program was started, giving kids all over the United States a chance to learn useful job skills while helping their communities.

In 1995, Mr. Duca began work on the Fitz Lane statue. This work was not commissioned, but a gift from Duca to the City of Gloucester. He worked on the piece for two years. Sadly, Duca died after finishing the smaller clay version; however, the large bronze statue that now looks out over Gloucester's waterfront was completed and dedicated in August 1997. A compelling tribute for both artists.

What's in a name?

It is commonly believed that Fitz Lane's full name was Fitz Hugh Lane – it is even shown on this memorial statue. However, it was uncovered by Jane Walsh of the Gloucester Archive Committee, that his middle name was changed to Henry when he was still a child. So scholars have had it wrong for over 100 years and the inscription on his memorial is incorrect.

Right:
The view Lane would have had from this hill is now interrupted by buildings on the active waterfront.

Lane at work drawing a landscape scene.

18

Gay City Ghost Town

Hebron, Connecticut

Nestled along Route 85 in Hebron, Connecticut, you'll find Gay City State Park. There are abundant hiking trails, a sandy beach to lounge on, youth group camping sites, a pond to swim and fish in, and picnic areas for meeting and eating. It is a lovely spot to enjoy some of the best of New England's outdoor activities. In such a beautiful spot, it may surprise you to learn that you are at the site of a lost civilization wasting away in the forest. Just off the White Trail is the ghost town known by the names "Gay City" and "Factory Hollow," a place that some would consider doomed.

In 1796, fleeing the dominant Congregationalist Church of Hartford, Elijah Andrus sought his own version of religious freedom. A devout Methodist, Andrus desired to incorporate a new town in which he could worship in peace. When he came upon a piece of land cradled between the shores of Still Pond and Black Ledge River, and felt the calmness of the spot, he knew that he had found a new home.

A total of twenty-five families, most belonging to the Gay family, settled on the site, and a small village quickly sprang up. With three saw mills on the Blackledge River, a textile mill by the pond, a blacksmith shop, distillery and many small homes, "Factory Hollow" had been born.

Right from its incorporation, Factory Hollow residents found themselves living a life separate from the towns around them. Largely due to religious differences, they distrusted outsiders and tried to remain on their own land. Reverend Henry Sumner, the town's spiritual leader, issued a decree that all residents must attend church services twice a week and even provided rum and other hard liquors to the men to increase attendance. Impassioned by the sermon, and the spirits, fights among the congregation were frequent. Quarrels between neighbors arose and hostility grew. Before long, many, including Andrus and his family, moved on to live in other nearby towns, forgoing some of their religious affiliations for the sake of a more peaceful existence.

Above from left:
Once the main road through town, now a rocky trail.

The river which drew individuals to Gay City to settle and build factories.

Nature is trying to reclaim this area of the Gay City Ghost Town.

Opposite:
The length of the former mill site is as long as a standard football field.

In 1811, Reverend Sumner and William Strong built a woolen textile mill. Processing fleece from the sheep on nearby farms, as the Hollow was too rocky to sustain many animals of its own, the mill churned out fabric that was sold for profit back in Hartford. It was a quite successful venture until the onslaught of The War of 1812, when the British blockades effectively halted all commerce in the area. The mill closed its doors.

Revived briefly as the Lafayette Manufacturing Co., the mill continued to operate until it mysteriously and inexplicably burned to the ground in 1830, leaving only the stone foundation remaining. Revived again by Reverend Sumner's son as a paper mill, it was marginally successful until the days of the Civil War. So many of the town's young men had enlisted, and never returned, that the rate of production waned greatly.

Though the population of the town had dwindled, its prime location to water sources continued to make it a valuable commodity. In 1870, a great paper mill was planned on the site of the former textile mill. Needing copious amounts of water with which to turn a great wheel, town residents and workers from surrounding areas began to dig a trench a quarter of a mile long and ten feet deep to divert water from Still Pond to the mill. When an optical illusion gave the appearance that the water was flowing uphill to the site, many of the superstitious workers quit on the spot, moving away and taking their families with them.

In her poem, "Gay City", Agnes Jones Staebner wrote:

They say a hundred years ago
A laborer cried his luck was ill,
Saying "It's Devil's work I know
To make free water run uphill!"

Ultimately, the mill was completed and survived several fruitful years before it too inexplicably burned to its very foundation in 1879. Even the most sensible residents gave into bouts of superstition and considered the land "cursed." The last of the families moved away, some disinterring their family members from the small village cemetery. The houses crumbled where they stood and the land remained largely unused until Emma P. Foster, a distant resident of the Gay Family, left the land to the State of Connecticut with the stipulation that the property be called "Gay City" and be used as a nature and wildlife preserve.

All that remains on the property is the large mill foundation, with square sluiceway opening, a few scattered house foundations, and a tiny graveyard near the entrance to the park. That does not stop the locals from continuing to spin yarns and tell tales of the long-ago town. Many believe the park to be haunted and point to two events in Gay City's history as their genesis.

It is believed that shortly before the Civil War a traveling jeweler, who frequented the villages in the area, was killed. He was robbed of his cash and wares and unceremoniously dumped in a charcoal pit at the edge of town. His body was found some time later, decomposed to a skeletal state, and the crime remains unsolved to this day. His murderer was never brought to justice and the unsettled spirit of the jeweler is still said to be searching for his revenge. Many have claimed to have seen a ghostly apparition near the former charcoal pit or the image of a walking or floating skeleton by the park's borders.

Another black spot on the town's history, also dating to around the time of the Civil War, involved the town's blacksmith. As the story goes, the blacksmith became irate when his teenage apprentice arrived very late to work. Flying into a wild rage, he chopped the boy to bits using a butcher knife. Some say that he was decapitated completely. Again, the murderer was said to have escaped punishment and the boy's restless spirit remains at the site. Over the years, sightings of a boy running quickly through the forest, as if late to be somewhere, have been numerous. Some of these witnesses claim the boy appears to be carrying his own head.

Whether purely works of fiction or overactive imaginations, Gay City is now an attraction for ghost hunters and paranormal enthusiasts. Electronic Voice Phenomena, the presence of a black mist hovering over the trails, disembodied footsteps and voices, temperature fluctuations, phantom smells, and the sudden onset of headaches have all been reported during formal investigations of the property. Several paranormal investigation teams have shared what they feel is "evidence" and released statements with the position that the location is, indeed, haunted.

On our excursion, we captured several orb photographs near the sluiceway and experienced the sensation of being "watched." Neither conclusive of a haunting, of course, but when you add it to the experiences of others over the past 100 years, it does give one cause for pause. Whether there are actual spirits plaguing the area, it is clear that "Factory Hollow" or "Gay City" is a "ghost" of its former self. The paths once tread by those seeking religious freedom, or just steady employment, are now replaced by hikers and bikers. Inch by inch, nature seeks to reclaim the land carved out of it, and minute by minute, it comes closer to success.

> The woods closed in on each redoubt
> Shoulder to shoulder with the sun
> When the last candle flickered out,
> The town was lost – the woods had won."

~Agnes Jones Staebner
"Gay City"

Author Notes

We had the privilege of exploring the park on an exceedingly rare September day where the weather was in the mid 80s and humid. The leaves were bright and many other visitors were also out and enjoying all that the park had to offer. We saw everything from a large equestrian group riding along one of the trails and then using one of the picnic areas to have a nice barbeque while their horses grazed nearby, as well as rows and rows of white chairs set out ready for beautiful fall wedding.

What we did not find as easily, was the old mill site. There were several reasons for this: we visited toward the end of the biggest hiking season and the map box was empty, so we were forced to rely upon the maps at the trailheads throughout the park. We selected the course that appeared to get us to the area of the mill ruins the most quickly, only to walk approximately a mile into the woods to a trailhead map indicating that we were on a completely different trail than the previous marker had indicated. We had followed the blazes the entire way and were sure we hadn't deviated. Later, we were able to validate that the two maps were not identical, which caused the confusion and amounted to just shy of an unneeded three-mile hike through some fairly swampy (aka buggy) terrain.

Our advice? Skip the maps all together! It's an amazing site and you *do* want to see it, so here is the easiest way. When you enter the state park, drive as far as you can, heading toward the beach. Park where you find a lot and walk down to the water's edge. Turn to your left and walk, keeping the water to your right, toward a small bridge in the distance. Long before you get to that bridge, you will see a sign with an arrow pointing toward the mill location on your left. There is great hiking throughout the state park as well, but if you're into ghost towns and ruins, toss the maps, follow our directions and you won't be a sweaty mess when you got there like we were!

~Summer

65

The opening where the water that "ran uphill" would have entered the former mill site. Seen in the opening is a light anomaly that paranormal investigators often refer to as "orbs."

19

P.T. BARNUM AND TOM THUMB
Bridgeport, Connecticut

The noblest art is that of making others happy.

~P.T. BARNUM

Time changes everything. What has previously been considered acceptable, or even beneficial, can be thought of by another generation as cruel and degrading. A prime example of how our belief systems change over time is found in the "Freak Show." Freak shows started off as exotic menageries or humans with unusual physical traits. As time passed, the general public became increasingly aware that these mysterious anomalies weren't weird human monstrosities, but actual humans with either a disease or some genetic mutation. Suddenly, when faced with the truth about many people's situations, they were no longer a fascination to be gawked at, but humans who to be pitied.

Modern freak shows became more focused on other types of freaks. Many are now performances of weird feats, such as hammering a nail up one's nose (heck of a sinus treatment), fire eating, sword swallowing, or people walking or sleeping on beds of nails. Instead of people being seen as having deformities (i.e., little people, bearded women), the human oddities are often people who have had extreme body modification, such as piercing, tattoos, or implants. Implants can range from beads placed under the skin in any configuration, to having silicone inserted in the shape of horns on the head. There is also "surface piercing," a piercing that runs under the skin on an area (i.e., the sternum) that is not protruding (i.e., the earlobe).

Now we have a new version of the freak show: reality television. We can choose to watch, in the privacy of our living rooms, everything that could have been seen in one of the old-time freak shows and much more. Though things have changed on the circuit, there is one thing that hasn't changed: the most famous showman of all time, P.T. Barnum, and his most famous act, General Tom Thumb.

Phineas Taylor Barnum was born in Bethel, Connecticut, on July 5, 1810. Barnum grew into a cunning businessman. As a young man, he juggled several businesses, from a general store to running a statewide lottery network and publishing a weekly paper. Not surprisingly, Barnum was quite controversial in his editorials and ended up spending two months in jail for libel. In 1834, his main source of income, the lotteries, were banned in Connecticut. Barnum packed up his family, sold his store, and moved to New York City. Once in New York, Barnum began his career as a showman. His first act was an old blind slave woman, Joice Heth, who he'd purchased from promoter R. W. Lindsay. Heth claimed to have been George Washington's nurse and to be 160 years old.

In 1841, Barnum purchased Scudder's American Museum and changed the name to Barnum's American Museum. It was set up as a family-friendly attraction that featured a zoo, wax museum,

lecture hall, and (of course) a freak show. The museum was the base of his operations. While showing Joice Heth, Barnum learned to extend the profitability of an act by taking it on the road. Once the crowds of New York became jaded to an act, he could send his shows to new venues for new crowds to amuse. Barnum's acts were incredibly diversified, from his first famous hoax creature, the "Feejee Mermaid," a combination of a fish's tail and the head and torso of a monkey, to Jenny Lind, a Swedish opera singer. In 1871, he began P.T. Barnum's Grand Traveling Museum, Menagerie, Caravan, and Circus. The circus was a replacement for his New York Museum that had burned down twice, once on July 13, 1865, then again on March 2, 1868. The second loss was too much for Barnum, who left the museum business and began with the traveling circus. In 1872, he changed it to "The Greatest Show on Earth." Then in 1881, Barnum partnered with James Bailey, the manager of the Cooper and Bailey Circus, to create Barnum and Bailey's. This was the first three-ring circus.

P.T. Barnum was known as the "Prince of Humbugs," a title he proudly embraced. He believed that a little humbug, something designed to mislead and deceive, was fine in promotions or ads, as long as the public was getting value for their money. He became an ardent debunker of many spiritualist mediums and spirit photographers. Barnum even wrote a book, The Humbugs of the World (1865), to expose the tricks used by mediums to defraud their clients.

Perhaps less well known about Barnum is that he was a vocal advocate against slavery. His museum often had performances of pro-abolitionist plays, such as a version of Uncle Tom's Cabin, or minstrel shows that satirized white racial attitudes. He was also a philanthropist, giving money to The Department of Natural History at Tuft's University and the Department of Public Works in the town of Bridgeport, Connecticut, where he served as mayor for a year. Barnum additionally donated the remains of Jumbo the Elephant, one of the favorite attractions in his traveling circus, to several different institutions. Jumbo's skeleton went to the American Museum of

Above from left:
A life-size personification of Tom Thumb at the Mountain Grove Cemetery in Bridgeport, Connecticut.

A tribute to Tom Thumb.

The final resting place of P.T. Barnum.

Natural History, while his stuffed hide went to Tuft's University, where it was displayed until it was destroyed in a fire in 1975.

In 1890, Barnum suffered a stroke and died on April 7, 1891, at the age of 80. When he died, he was one of the most famous Americans in the world.

He has remained a large part of the American mythos, and even people who don't know P.T. Barnum are familiar with his plethora of witticisms:

- "Nobody ever lost a dollar by underestimating the taste of the American public."
- "Never give a sucker an even break."
- "There is a sucker born every minute."

Barnum's spirit very much lives on in America. Of all the acts that Barnum promoted, there is one that stands above all the others (pun not intended). Charles Sherwood Stratton was born on January 4, 1838. Stratton was born weighing nine pounds, six ounces, and during the first six months of his life, he grew normally. At six months, he was twenty-five inches tall and weighed fifteen pounds; however, that was pretty much the end of young Charles' growth until 1847. At his tallest, he was about three feet, four inches tall.

When Charles Stratton was five years old, he met P.T. Barnum who taught him to sing, dance, and do impressions of famous people. Barnum took him on a tour of the U.S. and billed him as General Tom Thumb. The American tour was a success, and in January of 1844, Barnum took Charles on a tour of Europe. This tour was also hugely successful and Charles even appeared before Queen Victoria twice. Their success followed them throughout Europe and they returned to America triumphant.

General Tom Thumb continued to perform across America and Europe and he was quite successful. He even found love. Sometime in the early 1860s, he met Lavina Warren (also small), who worked for Barnum, as well. They fell in love and were married in a lavish, highly publicized wedding on February 10, 1863. Married at Grace Church in New York City and having the reception at the Metropolitan Hotel, there were over 2,000 guests. They even visited President Abraham Lincoln during their honeymoon. The couple continued to perform, and even toured Australia, Japan, and Europe together. Charles died suddenly on July 15, 1883 from a stroke.

The life-sized statue of Tom Thumb was purchased by P.T. Barnum and it was placed as part of his monument at Mountain Grove Cemetery in Bridgeport, Connecticut. Stratton's gravesite is located just yards away from where Barnum is buried.

AUTHOR NOTES

We visited the graves of these two men on a May evening, and the cemetery had been invaded by migrating geese. So, it was pretty funny trying to drive towards the back of the cemetery through the squawking crowds (and trying to avoid running over any of the very-annoyed birds). All I could think was how pleased Barnum would be at the loud crowd greeting visitors. It did seem strange to me that a man such as Barnum, the consummate showman, would have a site as simple as this one is. It is a beautiful family marker with just a simple marker for Barnum with the epitaph:

NOT MY WILL BUT THINE BE DONE

Tom Thumb's grave is a bit more grand with the high pedestal and life-sized statue; but, unfortunately, being more noticeable has lead to vandals smashing the original statue in 1959. It was restored with funds raised by the Barnum Festival Society and Mountain Grove Cemetery Association. There is a plaque on the monument noting the destruction and repair. As sad as it is to hear of the damage done to the statue of Charles Stratton, it is heartening to think that these two men, who were reportedly so close and instrumental in each other's success, are forever near to each other. It is also a benefit for those who wish to pay respects to the Prince of Humbug and his great jester.

~Cathy

VISITORS' INFORMATION

The cemetery is located at 2675 North Avenue in Bridgeport. If you go in through the main gate, drive straight back near to the end of the cemetery. Barnum's grave is obscured from the road by bushes, but Tom Thumb's Grave is about 100 feet past Barnum's site. I recommend finding the Tom Thumb statue, then looking in the same direction he is looking. That is where you will find P.T. Barnum.

20
MONUMENT SQUARE
Portland, Maine

Standing tall and proud in the eponymously named Monument Square in downtown Portland, Maine, the Our Lady of Victories Soldier's and Sailor's Monument honors "Portland's Sons Who Died for the Union." Dedicated on October 28, 1891, and added to the National Register of Historic Places in 1998, the statue is one of the most recognizable works of public memorial art in the Pine Tree State. Situated on the site of Portland's first City Hall and Public Market, it remains a worthy commemoratory "to those brave men of Portland."

The bronze Greco-Roman-style sculpture depicts the Roman Goddess of both war and wisdom, Minerva. Designed by acclaimed Maine native sculptor Franklin Simmons – the artist also responsible for the nearby remarkable depiction of Henry Wadsworth Longfellow from a plaster cast – he executed this work in his Rome, Italy studio. The figure stands soberly with a sword and a shield at the ready. This combines with the granite base and the bronze figures depicting Civil War era soldiers and Naval sailors, architect Richard Morris Hunt's contributions to the tribute.

Our Lady of Victories Soldier's and Sailor's Monument in Portland, Maine.

21

MERCY BROWN
Exeter, Rhode Island

When considering whether vampires may exist in America, one's first thoughts do not stray far from the southern states. Anne Rice's 1976 novel *Interview With the Vampire*, Charlaine Harris' *Sookie Stackhouse* series, and the *True Blood* television series it inspired, have firmly ingrained a modern-day mythos in which vampires exist almost exclusively in the southern states. In the heavily superstitious times of the early 19th century, however, northern vampires were not just creatures of legend and lore, but something that could be lurking just outside one's own front door. Unlike their bloodsucking counterparts, New England vampires were thought to be the deceased able to prey upon their living friends and family members – not by rising from the dead to feed; rather, from the confines of their coffins, slowly draining the life force from their loved ones. The only cure for such vampirism was to ritualistically dig up the corpse and mutilate the alleged vampire's remains. As barbaric as that sounds, the belief in pseudoscience surrounding the supernatural was strong and the practice was common place, with nearly twenty documented instances of these "remedies" being performed in New England even prior to the American Revolution.

Sickness was rampant in New England in the late 1800s and the most well-remembered New England family to be hit by the "Vampire's Grasp" was the Brown family of Exeter, Rhode Island. George and Mary Brown were simple farmers and the parents of three children: daughters Mary Olive and Mercy, and a son, Edwin. Mary was the first to be struck with the sickness, which we now believe to be consumption or tuberculosis, and she passed away in 1883. Mary Olive fell ill with the same sickness and passed the following year, in 1884, at just 20 years of age. Poor George buried both his wife and eldest child in the Chestnut Hill Cemetery within a year of each other. For many others in the community, it was much the same story. Consumption continued to run rampant through Exeter and the neighboring towns and there was little that Dr. Metcalf, the local physician, could do

Opposite:
The Brown family plot.

71

to stop it. George was given a reprieve for several years before Edwin began to literally, and suddenly, waste away before his father's eyes. Dr. Metcalf recommended that Edwin and his wife move to a well-known spa in Colorado Springs that would help abate his symptoms. Though the drier air did seem to slow down the progress of the consumption, which he had undoubtedly contracted from exposure to his family and neighbors, his health problems had, indeed, followed him west. Back in New England, Mercy had also contracted consumption. The disease was progressing quickly and Edwin hurried home to be by her side when she passed on January 18, 1892, at the age of 19. Since she had passed in the dead of winter, and the ground was frozen too solid to bury her properly, she was temporarily placed in the small receiving crypt of the cemetery where her mother and sister were already buried.

Shortly following his sister's death, Edwin's health took a turn for the worse and Dr. Metcalf proclaimed that his end was near. George took the news quite hard and his grief was amplified when the other villagers suggested that Edwin was suffering from Vampire's Grasp and that Mercy was preying on him from the crypt. Though they argued that the only way to save Edwin was to perform the folk ritual, he was hesitant. He held his neighbors at bay for a time, but in the end, he felt that his hands were tied. Ultimately, he gave his consent to allow the plots of not only Mercy, but also Mary and Mary Olive to be exhumed to look for symptoms of vampirism.

On March 17, 1892, Dr. Metcalf, with a group of townspeople, went to the Chestnut Hill Cemetery. George was grief stricken and not in attendance. The graves of Mary and Mary Olive were exhumed first, and their bodies were found to be in an advanced state of decomposition, as was expected given that they had been in the ground for nearly a decade. When Mercy's coffin was opened within the crypt, Dr. Metcalf found the following as reported in the *Providence Journal* on March 19, 1892:

> Dr. Metcalf reports the body in a state of natural decomposition, with nothing exceptional existing. When the doctor removed the heart and the liver from the body a quantity of blood dripped therefrom, but this he said was just what might be expected from a similar examination of almost any person after the same length of time from decease. The heart and liver were cremated by the attendants. Mr. Brown has the sympathy of the community.

Even though Dr. Metcalf's medical opinion was that Mercy was in a state of natural decay, this was not enough to dissuade the townspeople from completing the ritual. They took the heart and liver from Dr. Metcalf, burned it upon a rock in the cemetery and brought the ashes to George who mixed them with water and fed them to Edwin. Of course, this failed to provide a cure for the disease, nor effective relief from its symptoms, and Edwin passed away just six weeks later on May 2, 1892.

Though Mercy certainly was an average young woman and not a vampire, she is credited with inspiring the works of such notable authors as H.P. Lovecraft and Bram Stoker. Stoker's *Dracula* was written five years after Mercy passed, and newspaper clippings of stories about her were found in his personal effects. This notoriety, coupled with the tragic series of circumstances that lead to the mistreatment of her corpse, makes her plot the most frequently visited in the Chestnut Hill Cemetery – so much so, that her tombstone now has a heavy metal bar securing it after it was stolen from the cemetery in 1996.

So, if you stop to pay your respects, feel free to bring a trinket for her to mark your visit – just be sure to leave what is already there behind. Sweet Mercy and her family have lost enough.

VISITORS' INFORMATION

The Chestnut Hill Cemetery is located just behind the Chestnut Hill Baptist Church on Route 102 in Exeter, Rhode Island. Enter the cemetery and drive down the road through the center of the cemetery. The Brown family plot is nestled beneath a large tree, just to the left of the road. The receiving crypt and the stone upon which Mercy's organs were cremated following her disinterment are against the stone wall at the right-hand side of the cemetery.

Opposite:
The final resting place of Mercy Brown's body, Exeter, Rhode Island's "vampire."

The receiving crypt from which Mercy Brown was pulled and desecrated.

22
DR. SMITH'S GRAVE WITH A VIEW
New Haven, Vermont

A "dead ringer" that was "saved by the bell."

...common place enough sayings in the modern vernacular, but for many people, these sayings hint at one of the most basic and primal fears of all. Taphophobia, the fear of being buried alive, has severely crippled individuals from all walks of life. Even America's first president, George Washington, was said to have asked his family, friends, and closest advisors to delay burying him for three days after his passing, just in case he was not actually deceased.

Taphophobia has also been prominently featured in the works of artists, filmmakers, and authors throughout history. Wilkie Collins, Gertrude Atherton, and Bram Stoker all played with this fear in their early works. Edgar Allen Poe wrote three of his most well-remembered stories containing elements of taphophobia, "The Fall of the House of Usher," "The Cask of Amontilado," and "The Premature Burial." Modern explorations of the them have included the 2010 film *Buried*, starring Ryan Reynolds, that was set entirely in a wooden casket that was buried in the Iraqi desert with the main character entombed and very much alive. The movie was filmed chronologically, following the plot of the story, and the casket was slowly filled with sand. Reynolds was quoted as saying that on the last day of filming, shooting his final scenes was "unlike anything [he] had ever experienced in [his] life" and that he "never ever wanted to experience it again."

Perhaps this fear is not without merit, as history has provided many documented cases of individuals being buried before they had taken their final breath. Even with the advances in modern medicine, misdiagnose and misidentification can happen. One such case occurred in 1993, when a 40-year-old Coney Island woman was

Above:
Evergreen Cemetery in New Haven, Vermont.

Opposite:
The unnatural mound with concrete covered stairs where Dr. Smith and his wife were buried.

declared dead by an EMS crew and was later treated and released from the Coney Island Hospital after a Doctor heard a soft gurgling sound coming from her corpse, which was sealed in a bag in the hospital morgue. Even as recently as 2001, a woman was found lifelessly limp in a Boston bathtub with swollen and distended skin and limbs and unresponsive eyes. A suicide note and evidence of a drug overdose were discovered nearby. Only after being taken to the local funeral home, was it discovered that she was, in fact, still alive. As the funeral home director was locking the premises up for the evening, he thought he heard someone lightly breathing in the morgue and discovered that she still had a faint pulse. When you consider what could have happened had he received a phone call, a car drove by, or any other manner of noise were to have occurred, it is easy to see why some may legitimately fear that they could be buried too soon.

As of the date of the writing of this book, the United States Patent and Trademark Office has recorded more than twenty distinct variations of the theme of a "rescue" or "safety"-style coffin with features directly designed to allow the saving of its occupant in such a situation. Likely the most comprehensive model design was filed in the 1970s by Angelo Hays, who included a food locker, built in oxygen supply, books to read, a toilet, shortwave radio, and enough headroom to enable the occupant to sit up. His motivation for developing the safety casket? He himself had been buried alive for several days in 1937 and would have perished had insurance inspectors not ordered his body exhumed for unknown "insurance purposes." Though there are no known instances of one of these so-called "safety caskets" actually sparing someone from this fate, that hasn't stopped individuals from taking measures to decrease the likelihood of their need. In 1893, in the small town of New Haven, Vermont, the town physician designed one of the most elaborate tombs locals had ever seen, all in an effort to pacify his own taphophobia. In doing so, he created one of the most recognizable plots in all of New England, and possibly the country. (I know that it sounds a stretch ..... but oh well!)

A "Grave With A View"

Dr. Timothy Clark Smith, 1821-1893, studied medicine at the University of New York following stints as a teacher, merchant, and Treasury Department clerk. He was a well-regarded member of the community who became a staff surgeon in the Russian Army, and then as a U.S. Consulate at Odessa, Russia, followed by Galatz, Romania. A taphophobic from an early age, his medical training and exposure to other cultures only amplified his fear that he would contract the "sleeping sickness" – giving him the appearance that he had passed in his sleep, when he was still very much alive. He commissioned a two-room crypt to be built at his family's plot at the Evergreen Cemetery in New Haven, Vermont, for him and his wife. Though his wife's space was quite traditional in size and scope, Dr. Smith's was anything but. Above a slab, which would serve as the doctor's final resting place, rose a six-foot-tall pipe that was topped with a square concrete capstone containing a fourteen-inch square sheet of thick glass. The goal of this window, of course, was to allow visitors to the site a view of Dr. Smith, and he of them, in the event of a premature burial.

Local Lore

Like any good cemetery story, Evergreen is reportedly haunted by those who were not as prepared as Dr. Smith. The cemetery reputedly is home to several confused spirits who were buried before their time. Visits to the cemetery in search of these spirits have become a recreation of sorts for thrill seekers in the areas, especially on Halloween, his purported death date. Though the March 3, 1893 *Middlebury Register* newspaper printed an obituary indicating that Dr. Smith actually passed away on February 25, 1893, "suddenly" at the Logan House Hotel, where he had been living, that just wasn't as great of a story. Though the family plot contains the markers for his parents and siblings, Dr. Smith and his wife are not represented on the stones, and this has helped to keep the erroneous date of passing in circulation.

Passing down from generation to generation, and becoming an intricate part of the New Haven folklore, is that for many years after the good doctor's demise, one was able to look down through the window and see his skeletal remains from atop the grass-covered mound. The local storytellers insist that nestled across his chest were a chisel and other hand tools, and that a small bell lay beside his head. They even add that if you visit the site, and are very quiet, you just may hear the tinkling of a bell wafting through the cemetery grounds from Vermont's original proponent of being "saved by the bell."

AUTHOR NOTES

When we stopped to pay our respects, we found a cemetery much like any other in New England. Behind a scrolling iron marquee bearing the cemetery's name, we drove our car onto the grounds and instantly spotted the Smith family plot, it being quite distinctive from the others in the area. Though we tried our hand at Necrovoyeurism, due to a great deal of condensation behind the glass block in the capstone, we were unable to see the doctor's remains. It's possible, with a spotlight of some kind, we may have been able to see further down the shaft, but with the sunlight and lush tree growth overhead, we were unable to see more than about two feet down. That being said, it is a lovely and peaceful cemetery and didn't give overt indications that it was haunted by Dr. Smith's, or anyone else's spirits, and the tinkle of bells were nary to be found.

~*Summer*

VISITORS' INFORMATION

The Evergreen Cemetery is located in New Haven, Vermont, not far north from the town of Middlebury, where many Internet sites erroneously place the grave of Dr. Smith. Take Route 7 into town and then Town Hill Road for a little over a mile. You should spot the cemetery on your left. As you enter the grounds, you should easily spot an unnatural looking grass-covered mound near the front of the cemetery. It is approximately midway between the entrance and exit roads.

Right:
The windowed capstone that Dr. Smith had installed.

23
HOPE CEMETERY
Barre, Vermont

New Hampshire may be "The Granite State." But Barre, Vermont is "The Granite Capitol of the World." It has been estimated that a third of the public and private memorials and monuments in the United States have been carved from Barre Grey Granite. The abundance of this raw material in the area has had a notable impact on how the community plans memorials for their deceased, and nowhere is this more notable than in the town cemeteries.

Though Hope Cemetery is one of three burying grounds in the small town, it is by far the largest and most well-known. Spanning over 65 acres and containing nearly 10,000 stones and plots, Hope Cemetery is more like an art gallery than anything else. With stones featuring everything from portraits, a soccer ball, a stuffed arm chair, and cat, to initials, tractor trailers, and bay windows, the stones reflect both characteristics of the deceased and the personal artistic sensibilities of the town stonemasons and carvers.

AUTHOR NOTES

When compiling our list of sites to visit, Hope Cemetery was perhaps the site that we were most excited to go. As fans of funerary art, the cemetery was something that we couldn't possibly fail to include. That being said, we really were not prepared for the views that we encountered when we arrived. Just the cemetery gates were awe-inspiring. This is not a cemetery. It's an outdoor art gallery, and to try to adequately put words to the images we encountered would be impossible. The art speaks for itself, and so we will let it.

~Summer

VISITORS' INFORMATION

The Hope Cemetery is located at 262 East Montpelier Road in Barre, Vermont. While there is no designated parking, the pathways are ample to allow you to pull over safely. Wander the cemetery to your heart's content, but be sure to allow yourself plenty of time. We were there for several hours, but saw only a fraction of what the location had to offer.

Above:
Two large granite sentries flank the gates to the world famous Hope Cemetery.

Both pages,

Top row from left:
Hope Cemetery in Barre, Vermont.

William and Gwendolyn Halvosa are buried side-by-side and the stone features a likeness of the couple in their bed.

A tribute for a fan of automobile racing.

Middle row:
A Bi-plane for an individual who had pursued a career as a pilot

A large memorial stone for the Palmisano family that drew inspiration from Michelangelo's "Pieta"

Art in stone.

Gieuseppe Donati's tombstone features a raised relief of a soldier smoking, with the image of a loved one appearing in the smoke.

Bottom row:
Unique pyramid-shaped stones

A modern-styled memorial for the Catto family.

Architectural features and angels can be found throughout the cemetery

79

24
MELVIN MEMORIAL
Concord, Massachusetts

When president Abraham Lincoln called for volunteers to fight in the Civil War, the young men of Concord, Massachusetts, answered the call. The Melvin family's four sons were among the volunteers. Although the youngest did not initially pass inspection to join the troops, being too young to join, on his sixteenth birthday, he was enlisted. Of the four Melvin brothers, only the youngest survived the war. Asa Melvin, the oldest son, died during the Battle of Petersburg on June 16, 1864. He was buried in a mass grave near Spotsylvania, Virginia. John Melvin died of dysentery on October 13, 1863, in the Military Hospital at Fort Albany, Virginia. His brothers Asa and Samuel were at his bedside when he died. Samuel Melvin was taken as a prisoner of war with five of his comrades, on May 19 1864, and died in the infamous Andersonville Prison on September 25, 1864. Only one of the five men survived the camp and he shared the daily chronicle Samuel kept on life in the prison.

James, the youngest of the brothers, prospered after the war. In 1897, he hired Daniel Chester French, a native of Concord and childhood friend of the brothers, to create a monument for the three men. His design is widely considered to be one of the finest memorials in New England.

Daniel Chester French sculpted *Mourning Victory* for the site. The statue depicts the personification of victory emerging from the marble. She is looking down at the graves before her and is draped in an American flag. The details of the flag are subtle and easy to miss. Her right arm is holding the flag above her head while the left arm is outstretched, holding a laurel branch. This position of arms was changed from French's first version for a better presentation of the memorial at the Sleepy Hollow Cemetery. The markers for Asa, John, and Samuel are flanked with benches so two people can sit facing both the memorial and *Mourning Victory*. For the architecture portion of the monument, Daniel Chester French collaborated with the architect, Henry Bacon, who designed the edifice containing the tablets, benches, and statue.

AUTHOR NOTES

There is so much to see in the Sleepy Hollow Cemetery (see Chapter 13). Even with all the famous people buried at the location, including Daniel Chester French, this monument is a huge stand out. The flowing lines of statue, the solid architecture of the edifice, and the thoughtful and subtle imagery of the monument make this my personal favorite.

~Cathy

Above:
Daniel Chester French's depiction of Victory.

The Melvin memorial, *Mourning Victory,* in Sleepy Hollow Cemetery. The memorial pays tribute to three local brothers who fought in the Civil War.

25

MALAGA ISLAND GHOST TOWN

Phippsburg, Maine

"You have a real way about you, you know that, Lizzie?"
"That's what my granddaddy says: a real way about me."
"What else does your granddaddy say about you?"
"That I'm the closest thing to glory he'll ever see on God's green earth. What does your daddy say about you?"

~FROM *LIZZIE BRIGHT AND THE BUCKMINSTER BOY*
BY GARY D. SCHMIDT

Imagine, if you will, that you have lived your entire life on a small island town, just off the mid-coast of Maine. Your parents grew up there, as did their parents, so on and so on, back generations and decades. It's an exceptionally close-knit community. Everyone knows everyone and they all function as an extension of your own family. You have little reason to travel beyond the borders of your town, or off the island at all for that matter, with any real regularity, as you are able to access all your basic necessities locally, besides, you're the type of person who can make a lot from a little.

To be fair, your town has suffered a considerable bit of name calling and criticism by residents of the next major big city on the mainland, and by those in the state's capitol. They see you as "hicks," uneducated island bumpkins, but you're largely unconcerned. You're happy living where you are. God is good, and has provided enough for you to scrape by. You have your freedom, and as far as you can predict, you have no reason to suspect that you won't continue the tradition of starting and raising your own family on the island, in the community that you love.

Above from left:
The Malaga Island Preserve and site of James McKenney's home. He was considered the "King of Malaga" because of his spokesman role for the islanders.

Malaga Island in the New Meadows River.

A view from Malaga looking towards Bear Island.

Opposite:
The north side of the island and sites of the holes of Henry Griffin, the first individual to settle on the island, and Eliza Griffin, a laundress and fisherwoman who was the head of her own household and brought in more income than any man on the island.

Now, what if I were to tell you that the community you love, and loves you in return, was viewed by the general population of the state as so deplorable and despicable that it warranted obliviation. Right off the map. Every home, building, store and school. Nothing would be spared and not a stone would remain unturned or a grave left in peace. Yes, the people in this community were regarded as so morally reprehensible that their deceased, all seventeen corpses in the town graveyard, were disinterred and unceremoniously dumped into five group caskets and removed from the premises. Their crimes? They were unsightly, poor, and of mixed race, all of which offended the summer residents of the surrounding areas. They simply did not meet "Vacationland" standards.

Governor Plaisted's Role

In 1912, Governor Frederick Plaisted arrived on Malaga Island, just off the rocky coast of Phippsburg, Maine, with eviction notices in hand. None of the mainland towns wanted to claim Malaga as belonging to them or residing in their waters, for fear of being financially responsible for monetary aid to its residents. Governor Plaisted told Benjamin Darling, a freed African American slave who served as a spokesperson of sorts for the community, that his white wife and their children, along with his all of his white, American Indian, and biracial neighbors must leave the island. They could take their homes with them, if they could float them to shore on their own, which some were successful in doing, but anything left would be burned or razed. The school was given to the community of Loud's Island and despite much protesting, the residents were eventually successfully evicted from the island. The group caskets were labeled with small tombstones, with only a number, and placed in the back row of Pineland's Cemetery in New Gloucester, Maine, and that was that. With the island graves disinterred, and all its residents removed, Malaga Island was vacated and has never been occupied since.

Lives Interrupted

To add to this great injustice, Governor Plaisted had several individuals, who were particularly "dangerous" because they exhibited "chronic pauperism," smoked tobacco, and drank tea, committed against their will to the Maine School for the Feeble Minded. Thanks to the Eugenics Movement, which was in full-swing at that time, these people were later sterilized, also against their will, to prohibit them from bearing children and creating "impure blood." They cited the fact that freed slaves were not quick to assimilate to "white middle-class ideals" as a sign of imbecility and an "inability to be taught" and wished to prohibit the dilution of "strong white genes" by creating children of mixed race. Sadly, several children and teenagers met the same fate after also being declared "feeble minded," despite their race, by making a single error and in turn failing a single test by not being able to identify a "telephone," having grown up on an island in which there were no telephones.

The Newbery Award winning children's book *Lizzie Bright and the Buckminster Boy* is based on these tragic events, and I've yet to meet an elementary-aged student who has read it who hasn't questioned whether the Malagites' treatment was ethical.

A Belated Apology

In April of 2011, Governor John Baldacci and the State of Maine House of Representatives issued a "Joint Resolution Recognizing The Tragic Expulsion of The Residents of Malaga Island, Maine in 1912 and Redirecting Ourselves to the Maine Ideals of Tolerance, Independence and Equality For All Peoples." A worthy sentiment, but perhaps it would have gone further to mend wounds had the descendents of the Malaga residents been notified that the statement would be or even had been issued. Unfortunately, no one heard about the government admitting to their wrongdoing until four to five months after the fact, when *Down East Magazine* published a story on it.

A Century Later

Speaking with many Phippsburg locals, I was dismayed at how many of them had not heard of Malaga Island or what had become of its residents. There is good reason why the saying "if you do not learn from history, you will be doomed to repeat it" is so often quoted. Hopefully, the centennial will bring some awareness to this important, though undoubtedly dark and dismal, time in New England's history.

Though Benjamin Darling's grandchildren, now in their seventh generation, have accepted Governor Baldacci's apology, and accompanied him on a trip to the island in October of 2011, there is no true way to fix bigotry. Baldacci unveiled a plaque acknowledging the events that occurred on the island and dedicated it as a place now on the Portland Freedom Trail.

AUTHOR NOTES

The property is now owned by the Maine Coast Heritage Trust and you are welcome to visit it, if you are able to get to it. There is no scheduled transportation to or from the island, unfortunately. If you plan to visit, the north end of the island is the easiest and safest place to land. There is a nice walking path that is approximately a mile long that will take you around the interior of the island and by many former home sites, but do watch out for poison ivy. From land, you should be able to see the island from Sebasco Point in Phippsburg, Maine, but there is something about standing on the rock and shell-filled shore of Malaga Island that really drives the story home. It's the worst kind of ghost town; one that was never supposed to be abandoned.

~*Summer*

From top:

The north end of the island, where it is safe to dock and explore. The shell-covered beach is also the former site of Jake Mark's home.

The island is now used by local fisherman for the storage of lobster traps and other fishing equipment.

26
PINELAND CEMETERY
New Gloucester, Maine

The Pineland Cemetery, in New Gloucester, Maine, is the final resting place for patients of the Pownal State School for the Feeble Minded who were not claimed by their families. Among the rows of small white markers, is a single row of stones unlike all the rest. Marked with a single date of "1912," nine stones mark a series of group graves belonging to victims of one of the most unjust incidents in the state's history. When the residents of Malaga Island, Maine, were forcibly evicted from their homes, the community burying yard was removed as well. Seventeen bodies were exhumed, placed in five large coffins, and transported to the Pineland Cemetery. Bones mixing with those of their neighbors, the residents were reburied, without fanfare, and without the dignity of properly marked graves. This has led to the sad circumstance of many of their names being lost to time, as was the case for Henry Griffin's five children and three children from the Easton family.

The first tribute to the Malagaites was placed by Elaine Gallant, a local who had heard of the sad story and wished to memorialize their loss. Raising funds by soliciting donations from her friends, family, and the historical society, she had a small stone marker erected near the graves.

Though the stone memorial was a step in the right direction towards its account of the atrocities, it failed to convey the full scope of the incident. It was not until a group of students and teachers from the middle school in Bath, Maine, studied the island as part of an Expeditionary Learning unit, that a more thorough account was commissioned and placed at the site. Though simple in design, it does make strides in making the public aware of Malaga's history, without glossing over the rougher parts.

Opposite:
Pineland Cemetery in New Gloucester, Maine.

Author Notes

We visited the cemetery on an unseasonably warm winter day. The sky was clear and bright and the stones were covered with freshly fallen slow. A sad and lonely spot, it is hard not to feel melancholy. Uncharacteristically, we found very little to discuss while there. The pervasive sadness of the cemetery lends itself to quiet reflection and we came and went with a quiet somberness, hoping that the Malagaites have finally found the dignity that they were denied in life.

~Summer

Visitors' Information

To get to the Pineland Cemetery, follow Route 1 into Yarmouth, Maine. Turn onto Route 115 West and then bear right on Route 231. Just after passing through Pineland Center, you will see the town's Webber Cemetery. Turn right onto a gravel road right before this cemetery and follow the road to the back.

88

Right from top:
The stones erected for the Griffin and Easton children and Calvin and Laura Tripp.

A memorial plaque erected by a group of students and staff from the Bath Middle School.

27

MASSASOIT MEMORIAL
Plymouth, Massachusetts

Great Sachem
of
the Wampanoags
Protector and
Preserver of the
Pilgrims
1621

Erected by the
Improved Order of Red Men
A grateful tribute
1921

Some time around 1911, Cyrus Dallin (November 22, 1861-November 14, 1944) was approached by the "Improved Order of Red Men" to create a statue to celebrate the 300th anniversary of the Pilgrim Colony in Plymouth, Massachusetts in 1920. Dallin was probably best known for his statue of Paul Revere at the Old North Church in Boston, Massachusetts, and the statue of the Angel Moroni on the Spire of the Latter Day Saints temple in Salt Lake City (which has been used as a model for many other Latter Day Saints temples

across the world). However, Dallin is also known for his Native American statues, such as *Signal of Peace* (1894), *The Medicine Man* (1899), and the *Appeal to the Great Spirit* (1909). So when commissioned to create a "fitting monument to commemorate that historic first year in the new world," it was really no surprise that he selected Massasoit as his subject. It was erected in 1922.

Massasoit Ousamequin was the leader of the Wampanoag Confederacy of native people when the Pilgrims landed in today's

Above:
Massasoit and, to the left, the pavilion which holds Plymouth Rock, Massasoit looks down onto the Plymouth Harbor.

Plymouth, Massachusetts. Massasoit first made contact with the English settlers through his envoy, Samoset. He soon met with the leaders of the colony. A treaty was signed between the settlers and the Wampanoag promising, to "abstain from mutual injuries," and it is widely known that if not for the aid of Massasoit and his people, the colony in Plymouth would have failed. Massasoit sought a treaty with the Plymouth colonists, mostly because of the falling population of the Wampanoag people. Due largely to Massasoit's efforts, the people of the Wampanoag and the pilgrim settlers maintained peace between the two disparate groups—although the expansion of the European settlers, both in numbers and in the amount of land they used, was becoming a source of strife.

In 1661, Massasoit Ousamequin died and his son, Wamsutta (Alexander), became leader of the Wampanoag. However, the English settlers believed he was conspiring with the Narragansetts and accused him of selling land without their approval, and he was taken into custody. He died in English custody of a "sudden illness" in 1662, and his brother, Metacomet (Philip), became leader of the tribe and the peace was maintained until 1675, when King Philip's War started. The rumors that Wamsutta was tortured and killed by the settlers were a contributing factor. The war ranged over most of New England until April of 1678, when a peace treaty was signed, although Metacomet had been killed in August 1676, and wasn't there to see peace return.

Cyrus Dallin won an Olympic Bronze Medal for Archery in 1904.

Wampanoag means "people of the first light." Massasoit means "Great Sachem."

The Massasoit Memorial in Plymouth, Massachusetts.

28
FISHERMEN'S MEMORIAL
Gloucester, Massachusetts

They that go down to the sea in ships, That do business in great waters, These see the works of the Lord, And his wonders in the deep.

~PSALMS, 107:23-24

Anyone who has read *The Perfect Storm*, or watched the movie based on the book, knows that fishing is a highly dangerous profession. When you are on the sea, there is always the risk of equipment failure, unexpected bad weather, or even just walking across a slippery, unsteady deck can be a risk to life and limb. The town of Gloucester, Massachusetts, has lost more than a few of its sons and daughters to the sea.

Gloucester started as an English settlement in 1623, but the life there was harsh and unforgiving, so the settlement was abandoned in 1626. As time went on, though the area was resettled, the people who lived there were not fishermen at first. Gloucester was a farming and logging community. Fishing slowly began to become the industry of the town. First they stayed close to shore. It wasn't until some time in the 18th century that the Fishermen of Gloucester ventured out to the Grand Banks, an area off Newfoundland. The Grand Banks has not only a large amount of fish, but also a wide variety of different species: swordfish, haddock, lobster, and scallops are a few of the possible catches. However, the further away from the shore one goes, the greater the danger – especially when you are hundreds of miles away from home and the only help you have is, if by chance, another ship is nearby, or to wait for the Coast Guard to be able to get to you.

However it is a, sometimes, profitable career, and for many, the excitement of being so isolated and being out in the elements is a great joy. Many fishermen have a passionate love for their profession and couldn't imagine doing anything else. With its long seafaring tradition, it should be no surprise that Glocester has a gripping cenotaph sculpture, a monument for a person or group of people whose remains are elsewhere, for the town's lost fishermen. The statue is a fisherman at the wheel of a ship, balancing on a sloping deck and decked out in oilskins. The pose of the man implies he is steering through a storm. He is facing out at Gloucester Harbor, toward a wall of names of all the townsfolk who have been lost at sea. Under the eight-foot statue, on a stone base, reads the inscription:

Above:
Built directly on the waterfront, the memorial includes a list of locals who have perished while employed in the fishing trade.

THEY THAT GO DOWN TO THE SEA IN SHIPS
1623-1923

A smaller plaque facing the street reads:

Memorial To The Gloucester Fishermen
August 23, 1923

The sculpture was commissioned for the 300th anniversary in 1923, designed by Leonard Craske, the statue but wasn't completed and installed until 1925. It is now the town's logo; the figure is painted on the signs welcoming travelers to Gloucester and is prevalent in all the town's literature.

AUTHOR NOTES

We visited the monument on a lovely sunny day and I was impressed with the beauty of the site. The statue is on Stacey Boulevard, right near the bridge leading out of town. But there is a lovely boardwalk that is lined with American Flags, and if you look down from the retaining wall, you can see people enjoying the beach and playing in the surf. You can also see the ships go sailing past. I found myself wondering if the men and women boating past the spot stop and think that someday their names may be on that wall bringing chills, or perhaps the joy of the sea is enough to keep those thoughts at bay.

~Cathy

This memorial has also been called, "Man at the Wheel."

The Gloucester, Massachusetts Fisherman's Memorial

29

THE NEW HAVEN HOLOCAUST MEMORIAL
and
THE NEW ENGLAND HOLOCAUST MEMORIAL
Boston, Massachusetts

The Holocaust

When Adolf Hitler became the Chancellor of Germany in 1933, it was impossible to predict that, in just over a decade, a genocide would be waged resulting in the murder of over six million Jewish people. Through the passing of a series of laws, the Nazis enabled the imprisonment and execution of people they considered "inferior" including the Jews, gypsies, Johovah's Witnesses, and homosexuals. Many were sent to concentration camps, while others fell victim to a "euthanasia" program. During peak operation, Hitler's "death factories" murdered thousands of innocents a day, and continued to do so until the U.S. and Allied Forces ultimately defeated them and liberated the remaining concentration camp survivors in May of 1945.

The New Haven Holocaust Memorial

In 1967, a group of about seventy families in the New Haven, Connecticut area expressed interest in honoring their loved ones who had perished during The Holocaust. Each week, each family donated a single dollar, and, in 1977, the country's first memorial to The Holocaust on public land was created.

Designed by lifelong New Haven resident Marvin Cohen, the New Haven Holocaust Memorial is centrally located in Edgewood Park and was designed with a heavy emphasis on symbology.

Rising from a base, in the shape of a Star of David, are six curved towers shaped of metal and barbed wire, symbolizing six

Above from left:
The glass towers of the The New England Holocaust Memorial are engraved with a close up of the numbers that were tattooed on the prisoners in the "death camps."

The numbers.

main prison camps. Beside the towers, along the base of the Star of David, are six evergreen Yew trees, representing the six million individuals who lost their lives there. This variety of tree was specifically selected because they remain green during the harsh New England winters and provide a spot upon which to reflect, no matter what season one stops to pay their respects. A plaque on the side of the memorial reads:

> We remember the six million Jews murdered by the Nazis during World War II 1939-1945 (5699-5705).
> Dedicated by the City of New Haven and the New Haven Jewish Federation

A complimentary plaque expresses a similar sentiment in Hebrew and nearby plaques honor the loss of life of other innocents during World War II, as well as the contributions of the Gentiles who assisted in rescuing Jews from the camps. Arguably the most unique aspect of the memorial is that it is not only in a place that commemorates an event in history, but it is also a final resting spot and grave. Buried at the center of the Star of David is a small box containing soil and ashes, presumably including human remains, which were recovered from the death camp at Auschwitz. This box was interred at the site during the groundbreaking of the memorial and makes the site unlike any other in New England.

Surrounding the memorial is a series of benches and plaques in a plaza setting. Here are listed the eighteen death camps operated by the Nazi regime. When we visited the memorial, we found that visitors had been observing the common cemetery tradition of placing small pebbles and stones upon these plaques to indicate that they had stopped to pay their respects. When you consider that this practice is commonly believed to have roots in the communal building in cairns, first recorded in the biblical story in which Jacob's sons each brought stones to mark their mother, Rachel's, grave, this felt strikingly appropriate. As this tradition predates the use of tombstones to mark graves, often, a pile of stones is all that would indicate that a tract of land was an individual's final resting place, and the communal marking of these spots align well with the overall purpose of the memorial site.

The New England Holocaust Memorial

Ilse, a childhood friend of mine,
Once found a raspberry in the camp
And carried it in her pocket all day
To present to me that night on a leaf.
Imagine a world in which
Your entire possession is
One raspberry and You gave it to your friend.

~NEW ENGLAND HOLOCAUST MEMORIAL

In 1995, a group of holocaust survivors who had settled in the greater Boston, Massachusetts area in search of new lives, desired a memorial to commemorate the immense loss of lives lost. Following an international competition with over 500 entries, the New England Holocaust Memorial was erected in the Faneuil Hall area of the city near the waterfront. Designed by Architect Stanley Saitowitz, of Johannesburg, South Africa, the site has won many awards, including the American Institute of Architects' Henry Bacon Medal for Memorial Architecture and the Boston Society of Architects Harleston Parker Award. The memorial site is maintained by the Boston National Historic Park system.

A series of six-foot-tall glass towers, etched with six million numbers suggestive of the infamous tattoos the Nazis inflicted on their victims, is placed along a black granite path. Internally lit, the towers glow day and night and is symbolically rich in detail. The monument features a recurring theme of items in groupings of "six." The six glass towers represent the primary Nazi death camps of Majdanek, Chelmno, Sabibor, Treblinks, Belzec, and Auschuwitz-Birkenau, and the names of these camps are engraved on the pathway below each tower. The symbol of the "six" can also be representative of the six million victims, the six years which accumulated the highest death toll, and the six menorah, or memorial candles. The granite pathway begins with an engraved stone reminding us to "Remember," written both in English and in Hebrew. Nearby, a marker indicates that the site was "built to foster memory of and reflection on one of the greatest tragedies of our time, the Holocaust (Shoah)."

Top from left:
The New Haven Holocaust Memorial.

The memorial is designed to be reminiscent of barbed wire.

A box containing human remains and soil from the Auschuwitz concentration camp are buried within the base of the memorial.

Left:
Auschwitz tributes.

As visitors walk through the towers, charred embers smoke and rise through stainless steel grates below each tower, evoking impressions of the gas chambers. Glass panels in the base of each tower include statements of personal experiences of The Holocaust, along with key events in the timeline of events. At the end of the pathway, we are again encouraged to "Remember," this time in both English and Yiddish.

The final sentiment that visitors to the memorial are sent away with is a poem by Pastor Martin Niemoeller, which has become associated with the over-arching lessons of The Holocaust:

> They came first for the Communists,
> And I didn't speak up because I wasn't a Communist,
> Then they came for the Jews,
> And I didn't speak up because I wasn't a Jew.
> Then they came for the trade unionists,
> And I didn't speak up because I wasn't a trade unionist.
> Then they came for the Catholics,
> And I didn't speak up because I was a Protestant.
> Then they came for me,
> And by that time no one was left to speak up.

Though, Pastor Niemoeller himself had delivered some anti-Semitic sermons early in the war, he later publicly opposed Hitler and was sent to a concentration camp. His message is as poignant and relevant now as ever and it is for this reason why continuing to create memorials that respectfully pay tribute to those we have lost remains of the utmost importance in a modern society.

AUTHOR NOTES

The New Haven Holocaust Memorial can be visited at Edgecomb Park, at the corner of Whalley Avenue and West Park Avenue. If you find yourself in the area, we encourage you to stop and pay your respects by leaving a stone on the center memorial or the camp markers, as we did.

The New England Holocaust Memorial is located in Carmen Park, situated along Congress and Union Streets and near Faneuil Hall. It is just steps from the Freedom Trail and is a must see while visiting the city.

Both of these memorials are shining examples of the best in urban monument design. They have successfully created quiet spots of reflection and remembrance of an exceedingly tragic series of events in world history in an otherwise busy urban environment. We hope that you will take the time when visiting these capital cities to visit these beautiful tributes.

~Summer

Above from left:
The New England Holocaust Memorial in Boston, Massachusetts.

Six glass columns.

The columns shine in the cityscape

Right:
Stones left in remembrance and tribute.

FLAGSTAFF MEMORIAL CHAPEL

30
FLAGSTAFF GHOST TOWN
Flagstaff, Maine

There's an old dirt road, just off route nine.
Fades into the lake, at the low water line.
Sometimes I wander down that road alone.
Remembering the town, that I once called home.
I grew up in the valley, every neighbour a friend.
Until the modern world started creeping in.
One day came the lawyers, with cash in hand.
They swore that our village would light up the land.

~SLAID CLEAVES
"BELOW"

When removing a bandage, is it better to peel it off slowly or rip it off quickly? This may seem an odd question, but it seems an apt metaphor for the what the people around Flagstaff, Maine, went through. In 1923, a bill was introduced to the Maine State Legislature proposing damming the Dead River, but it was not initially passed. The proposal was reintroduced, and, in 1937, the legislature authorized the creation of the Dead River Storage and renewed the act in 1939 and 1941. What this meant for the town of Flagstaff was that Central Maine Power Company (CMP) was given permission to dam the Dead River, not for a hydroelectric dam, but to create a backup reservoir for the five generating stations on the Kennebec River. The dam at Long Falls would create a lake that was about twenty-five miles long and would drown not only the town of Flagstaff, but also the village of Dead River and Bigelow Plantation. It would take over twenty-five years to get from the first proposal in 1923 to the flooding of the town in 1950. It was a slow and agonizing process for many of the townsfolk.

Above from left:
The lake in the fall.

The stained glass windows and bell were removed from the church in Flagstaff and placed in the Flagstaff Memorial Chapel in Eustis, ME.

A town no longer.

Opposite:
A town beneath a lake – the site of the former town of Flagstaff, Maine.

According to folklore, the names for the town of Flagstaff, Bigelow Township, and Bigelow Mountain all came from the ill-fated march on Quebec City. By the time the expedition made it to the Flagstaff area, they were wet, cold, tired, and half starved. Col. Timothy Bigelow climbed what we now call Bigelow Mountain, trying to catch sight of Quebec. All he could see from the area was mountains to the north and wilderness to the south. After the troops came back down to the Valley, they planted a flagstaff to mark the area.

Flagstaff was organized as a Plantation in 1865, with Dead River and Bigelow following in later years. Flagstaff was the unofficial center of the three, since it had the most businesses and the local high school. The people of the Valley were mostly lumbermen, guides, farmers, or worked at the sawmill. They were people who had a connection to their land. Many of the families had lived there for generations and it was hard for them to leave a place they'd always known.

Harder still, for some, was having to dig up the town's graveyard. Central Maine Power hired a crew to move the bodies of the dead, so that they would not be left behind when the water flooded the area. However grateful the residents were that CMP paid to have their dead moved to a cemetery in Eustis, Maine, it was still wrenching for them to see the graves of their loved ones disturbed. In the book *There Was a Land*, Ken Taylor, a native of Flagstaff, shares his experience moving the graves:

> They were paying four dollars an hour to move graves. We made wooden boxes three feet by two feet by one and one-half feet. We put the bones in there. They were carefully marked, of course. Most were reburied by the church in Eustis, but you could have your graves moved anywhere you wanted. We moved the stones and markers, too.
>
> At one time it was the custom to bury a person with woolen socks on his feet. One man, he had been dead for 20 to 30 years, still had those socks. In one grave of a little girl, we found a china doll.

FLAGSTAFF & DEAD RIVER CEMETERIES

Even though it was officially decided in 1937 to flood the area, work did not begin until the summer of 1948. This is when CMP began clearing the heavy timber from the area where the dam would be built. At about the same time the cutting started, a forest fire broke out. It is believed that some of the people hired to clear out the trees decided that fire would be a quicker solution. Over fifty acres of private forest was burned and the town almost went up in flames, but the town was spared, for a while. The fires meant that most people's recollection of their final summer in the valley involved the smoke and ash that covered the area.

By the time cutting began, Flagstaff had dwindled to about seventy people. The young people didn't want to stay, since they knew there would be no future, and those who were still around, were there just to work for CMP until the dam was built; then they planned to leave and find work elsewhere. For the elderly it was harder. Their roots were settled deep in this soil and the idea of leaving was more than most could bear. But in the winter of 1949, the Dead River had been dammed and its waters were backing up into the town. There were some diehard residents who had not sold their land to the company and had set up sandbags to stop the water from entering their homes, but eventually, even the most stubborn of residents were gone by the end of 1950.

The town has made occasional appearances in the land above water – most notably in 1979 when the water levels dropped so low that people could once again walk down the streets of Flagstaff and even see the remains of some of the homes that hadn't been removed before the flooding. It did give the people a chance to have one last look at their beloved town.

The road that once lead to a thriving community.

There is a particular sadness about towns that have been flooded. This isn't a place that people have left willingly. These people were taken from their town and exiled from the only home many of them had ever known. Cliff "Captain" Wing even suggested building an ark so that all the townspeople could still live in Flagstaff and remain a community. There are still reunions for the former townsfolk to get together, share memories, and renew old friendships. There are children who weren't alive who attend these gatherings, meeting other children with whom they might have grown up with, if their town had not been flooded all those years ago.

AUTHOR NOTES

The area around Flagstaff lake is now a beautiful recreational area. Many people come to stay in the towns of Eustis or Stratton while they enjoy the lake. You can even hire a boat to "show you around the town of Flagstaff" or some great fishing spots. There are plenty of snowmobile trails for the winter and hiking trails for the summer. It is also not far north of one of Maine's most famous ski resorts, SugarLoaf. The area is an outdoorsman's paradise, much the way it was before the flood.

~Cathy

Left from top:
The dam built by Central Maine Power Company.

Flagstaff Stone Caption:
The inscription on the back reads: "Mill Stone given on August 3, 2003 by Julian and Lelia Dunphy in memory of Ralph Dunphy, Benjamin Safford and Robert Tay

31

L. L. BEAN'S GRAVE
Freeport, Maine

Sell good merchandise at a reasonable profit, treat your customers like human beings, and they will always come back for more.

~LEON LEONWOOD BEAN

It should come as no surprise that one of New England's best-known companies sells outdoor gear. In New England, we have a wide variety of sporting activities that vary not only by region, but also by season. You can hike up the side of a mountain in the summer and then you can ski down it in winter . You can swim in the Atlantic Ocean in the summer or beachcomb during the winter. No matter the location or time of year, many New Englanders can be found spending the majority of their time outside, and for many of us, L. L. Bean is the supplier for all things *outdoorsy* (and not so *outdoorsy*).

It all started when Leon Leonwood Bean was born on October 13, 1872, in Greenwood, Maine. Even as a child, he was an outdoorsman and entrepreneur. As the story goes, when he was 9 years old, he was given a choice by his father to either sell steel traps or go to a local fair with his family. He chose to work, and that was his first sales experience.

At the age of 12 his parents died, within four days of each other, leaving young Leon and his five brothers orphaned. The boys moved to South Paris, Maine, to live with relatives. Leon worked wherever he could, selling soap, hunting, trapping, and doing assorted farm-work. He successfully killed and sold his first deer at the age of 13.

Leon married Bertha Porter in 1898, and they raised three children: two boys and a girl. Leon continued being an avid outdoorsman, but he found that the gear available to him was not good enough to meet his needs, particularly the boots. Nothing turns a pleasant trip in the woods into a miserable one faster than cold, wet, uncomfortable feet (well, maybe running into an angry bear). He decided he could design a pair of hunting shoes that would be warm, dry, and comfortable.

His "Maine Hunting Shoe" was created in 1912, and he sent out his first brochure aimed at Maine hunters. Bean guaranteed the quality of his shoes and, unfortunately, 90 of the first 100 boots were returned, since the shoes developed cracks in the rubber and began leaking. This was the rough beginning of the "Bean Boot." Undaunted by this, L.L. took out a loan for $400 and went to Boston where he convinced the United States Rubber Company to help him improve the quality of his boots. The revised boots became so popular that he was able to set up, in 1917, a storefront on Main Street, in Freeport, Maine. The flagship store and product line have grown beyond any possible expectations. L.L.'s philosophy of offering quality products at a reasonable price and his down-to-earth catalog descriptions have only risen in popularity.

On February 5, 1967, L.L. Bean died in Popano Beach, Florida, at the age of 94 years. He is buried in Webster Cemetery, on Webster Road, in Freeport, Maine. The cemetery is just a few miles away from the flagship L.L. Bean Store, still located on Main Street. The store that is his legacy still has members of his family involved with the business and has become a Maine institution. People come from all over the world to shop and just look around to see how it all started with a wet foot.

His gravesite is very much what one would expect, knowing about L.L.'s outlook on life. It isn't fancy. There is a marker for the family simply labeled "Bean" and small individual stones for each of the family members. There are no epitaphs and no embellishments; it is as straightforward as the man himself was. I had expected that there might be memorials left behind by admirers, but when your products are guaranteed, as L.L. Bean's still are, not many people are going to be leaving them behind.

AUTHOR NOTES

Okay, disclaimer time. I am an admitted L. L. Bean fan girl. I can't remember there being a Christmas in my family that there wasn't some gift coming from L.L. Bean. I even worked for the company as a seasonal employee for more than one year. I have many fond memories of shopping trips to L.L. Bean and can remember the fun of being allowed to be up late, past my bedtime, to hit the store during the overnight hours. (Nothing is more fun than wandering into the home department to see who has fallen asleep on one of the couches or chairs laid out for display.) So I was very keen to see the grave of the man who had started it all. I am pleased to have been able to pay my respects to the man, but, I must admit, that my Yankee frugality prevented me from leaving any L.L. Bean mementos as tribute. Perhaps, that dedication to his store's products is tribute enough?

~ *Cathy*

From top:
The Bean family plot.

The final resting place of L.L. Bean.

WHAT IS IN A NAME?

It is usually accepted that L.L. stood for Leon Leonwood. However, it is believed (and confirmed by Leon Gorman, L. L.'s grandson) that his middle name was actually Linwood, but someone misspelled the name as Leonwood and L.L. took a liking to it and officially adopted it as his name.

32

NATIONAL DAY OF
MOURNING MEMORIAL
Plymouth, Massachusetts

We are not vanishing. We are not conquered. We are as strong as ever.

~ MOONANUM JAMES
CO-LEADER OF UNITED AMERICAN INDIANS
OF NEW ENGLAND

For many Americans, Thanksgiving is a day of celebration. Many schoolchildren, at least in New England, have drawn a turkey from the shape of their hand and learned all about how the Pilgrims celebrated surviving their first year in the New World by having a feast and inviting some friendly Indians along. In schools, it is all very upbeat; however, there is another side to this story – a not so happy/upbeat version.

Not much thought is given to the native people, the Wampanoag, who helped the settlers survive in their new surroundings.

In 1970, a new event was established. According to the United American Indians of New England (UAINE) the first National Day of Mourning was organized after Wamsutta, Frank James, the leader of the Wampanoag Tribe, was asked to give a speech at a celebration of Thanksgiving at the 350th anniversary, sponsored by the Commonwealth of Massachusetts. When the organizers reviewed his speech, he was told it was too inflammatory for what they envisioned as a celebration of brotherhood. Wamsutta was given a revised speech by the planning committee of the event. Instead, he gathered with supporters near the Statue of Massasoit on Cole's Hill looking down on the Plymouth Rock Memorial where the Commonwealth's celebration would be held. Here, Wamsutta read his speech. Since that day, there has been an observance of The National Day of Mourning with a march through Plymouth, ending at Massasoit's statue. Here speeches are given, social time scheduled, and a potluck dinner shared later in the day. The monument acknowledging the National Mourning Day is on Cole's Hill near Massasoit's Statue. It reads:

In 2012, the Dallas Cowboys and the Washington Redskins played each other for the 7th time on Thanksgiving...

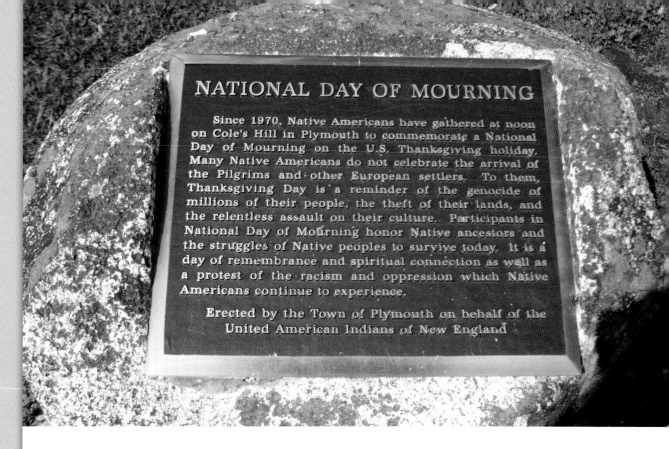

NATIONAL DAY OF MOURNING

Since 1970, Native Americans have gathered at noon on Cole's Hill in Plymouth to commemorate a National Day of Mourning on the U.S. Thanksgiving holiday. Many Native Americans do not celebrate the arrival of the Pilgrims and other European settlers. To them, Thanksgiving Day is a reminder of the genocide of millions of their people, the theft of their lands, and the relentless assault on their culture. Participants in National Day of Mourning honor Native ancestors and the struggles of Native peoples to survive today. It is a day of remembrance and spiritual connection as well as a protest of the racism and oppression which Native Americans continue to experience.

Erected by the Town of Plymouth on behalf of the United American Indians of New England

The National Day of
Mourning Memorial

Since 1970, Native Americans have gathered at noon on Cole's Hill in Plymouth to commemorate a National Day of Mourning on the U.S. Thanksgiving holiday. Many Native Americans do not celebrate the arrival of the Pilgrims and other European settlers. To them, Thanksgiving Day is a reminder of the genocide of millions of their people, the theft of their lands, and the relentless assault on their culture. Participants in a National Day of Mourning honor Native ancestors and the struggles of Native peoples to survive today. It is a day of remembrance and spiritual connection as well as a protest of the racism and oppression which Native Americans continue to experience.

There is a second marker located in Post Office Square. It reads:

METACOMET (KING PHILIP)
After the Pilgrims' arrival, Native Americans in New England grew increasingly frustrated with the English settlers' abuse and treachery. Metacomet (King Philip), a son of the Wampanoag sachem known as the Massasoit (Ousameqin), called upon all Native people to unite to defend their homelands against encroachment. The resulting "King Philip's War" lasted from 1675-1676. Metacomet was murdered in Rhode Island in August 1676, and his body was mutilated. His head was impaled on a pike and was displayed near this site for more than 20 years. One hand was sent to Boston, the other to England. Metacomet's wife and son, along with the families of many of the Native American combatants, were sold into slavery in the West Indies by the English victors."

Both markers were set up as part of an agreement between the Town of Plymouth and members of UAINE after a confrontation on Thanksgiving/National Day of Mourning.

33
FISHERMEN'S WIVES
MEMORIAL
Gloucester, Massachusetts

For those of us left behind, the vast unmarked grave which is home for those lost at sea is no consolation. It can't be visited, there is no headstone on which to rest a bunch of flowers... The only place we can revisit them, is in our hearts, or in our dreams. They say swordboatmen suffer from a lack of dreams, that's what begets their courage... Well we'll dream for you: Billy, and Bobby, and Murph, Bugsy, Sully, and Alfred Pierre... Sleep well... Good Night...

~Mary Elizabeth Mastrantonio
as Linda Greenlaw, in The Perfect Storm

Just across the bridge from the Fishermen's Memorial (see Chaper 28) on Western Avenue, in Gloucester, Massachusetts, is a monument that the Gloucester Fishermen's Wives Association (GFWA) has created.

In the words of Angela Sanfilippo, GFWA president:

The memorial serves as a testimonial to what wives, mothers, sisters, and children of fishermen of the world have endured because their men chose to be on the water. They had no choice but to stand on rock, to be on land.

The twelve-foot-high bronze sculpture shows a woman carrying a child in her arms, while an older boy clings to her skirt. All three are staring out at sea showing that even though they must continue with their daily lives, there is a part of them that is always thinking of their loved one who is beyond their reach.

Opposite:
A woman and her children eagerly await the
return of their fisherman.

The inscription around the base of the sculpture reads:

The wives, mothers, daughters and sisters of Gloucester fishermen honor the wives and families of fishermen and mariners everywhere for their faith, diligence, and fortitude.

The statue was designed by Leonard F. Craske in 1925, and is surrounded by tiles that are carved with the names of fishermen and their families.

AUTHOR NOTES

When we first went to Gloucester, we visited the Fishermen's Memorial, then left. We didn't realize that just down the street was this amazing monument. When we saw pictures of the memorial, we knew we had to head back to Gloucester to see this statue. We got into town around Sunset and the colors of the sky and the light reflecting off the statue was breathtaking. We ended up staying until after the sun had set, reading all the names on the ground. It is well worth a visit, and while you're there, be sure to stop off at the Harbor Loop to see the incredible statue of Fitz H. Lane. Gloucester does seem to be a city of impressive memorials.

~Cathy

The Fishermen's Wives Memorial in Gloucester, Massachusetts.

34

LEWISTON VETERAN'S MEMORIAL
Lewiston, Maine

Posterity – You will never know how much it has cost my generation to preserve your freedom. I hope you will make good use of it.
~JOHN QUINCY ADAMS

The above quote from John Quincy Adams is featured prominently at Veteran's Memorial Park in Lewiston, Maine. A large waterfront plot at the base of the falls of the Androscoggin River, this heartfelt tribute to Maine veterans is unique in that it honors all individuals who have served in the United States Armed Services, both living and deceased, serving in both times of war or of peace. Where many modern memorials are dedicated to the loss of life, Veteran's Memorial Park stands as a spot of quiet reflection within the second largest city in Maine. Formerly named Heritage Park, Joseph A. Paradis a Korean War veteran, Prisoner of War, and a Purple Heart recipient, obtained the land from the city with the specific intent of creating a public memorial, in 2001. Collette Monument Co., a third-generation family business, was charged with designing a fitting memorial, and utilized the latest advancements in stone carving technique to create highly detailed tributes, including *The Price of Freedom* featuring life-size depictions of service men and women in all branches of the U.S.

military. In 2004, the park finished its initial phase of development and opened to the public, with a large unveiling on Veterans' Day.

The park is also notable for the variety of memorials throughout its location. Just beneath a collection of service flags lies a semi-circle of marble tablets containing the names of over four thousand locals who honorably served the county. A laser-engraved key, featuring an image of the Statue of Liberty and the seal of the United States, sits in the center, assisting visitors in connecting with the names displayed. The park also contains memorial benches, a tribute to the "Gold Star Mothers," who have lost their children in military combat, a burial plot of tributes and trinkets left at the Vietnam Wall memorial in Washington, D.C., and an example of a "Willy's "Jeep" that was used in the Korean War.

"Remember The Maine," a 498-pound projectile that had been retrieved after 14 years from the bay in Havana, Cuba, where the U.S.S. *Maine* was attacked, stands beside a laser-inscribed stone. On the rear

Above:
The Lewiston, Maine Veteran's Memorial.

of the marker is a list of the names and hometowns of the five Mainers who were killed during the attack and resulting explosion.

On Veteran's Day 2010, several new additions to the park were unveiled, including a large Naval anchor, indicating that this land will continue to evolve and change in an effort to be more wide-reaching and inclusive. A small marker, in similar shape and size of a traditional tombstone, faces the waterfall and contains a carving of the Tomb of the Unknowns and "those known only but to God."

A five-inch, fifty-one caliber naval cannon, which formerly sat outside of the chapel at the now-closed Brunswick Naval Air Station, was mounted near the river's edge, ready to thwart any would-be attackers approaching from nearby Turner, Maine.

VISITORS' INFORMATION

The Veteran's Memorial Park is located at 2 Main Street, just to the Lewiston side of a bridge honoring former Lewiston mayor and Maine Governor James B. Longley. Though lovely year-round and at any time of day, the site is especially peaceful and poignant just after sunrise. For a more jubilant or aerial viewing, you may wish to visit the site during The Great Falls Balloon festival, held annually in August along both sides of the riverfront setting of the park. Take in a hot air balloon ride or participate in numerous musical, cultural, and entertainment opportunities suitable for all ages.

Right from top:
The Price of Freedom.

A memorial, and artillery shell from the U.S.S. *Maine*.

Opposite
An anchor at sunrise.

35

PLEASURE BEACH GHOST TOWN
Bridgeport, Connecticut

Every time we walk along a beach some ancient urge disturbs us so that we find ourselves shedding shoes and garments or scavenging among seaweed and whitened timbers like the homesick refugees of a long war.

~LOREN EISELEY

On June 16, 1996, a carelessly discarded cigarette butt, allegedly, ended an over-100-year old tradition. Pleasure Beach was an island/peninsula community. When the tide comes in, the strip of beach that connects the area to the rest of the beach returns to the ocean, straddling the town line between Stratford and Bridgeport, Connecticut. The community had been surviving since it was first built as an amusement park in 1892. From that time through 1947, the area thrived without a bridge, until one was built that year by the Army Corps of Engineers connecting Pleasure Beach to Stratford.

Pleasure Beach had a history of fires, as well. In 1953, part of the midway was destroyed by a fire started by faulty wiring. In 1957, the bridge between Pleasure Beach and Stratford was set on fire by a discarded cigarette. (Sound familiar?) In 1965, the bridge caught on fire, again. In 1972, a large portion of the amusement park's midway burned down. In 1973, The Ballroom burned to the ground. In 1996, the boardwalk between the bathhouse and beach area was burned by vandals. Then came the final bridge fire, in 1996, that burned 200 feet of the old wooden bridge. There have also been several occurrences of collisions with the bridge, since the area is a hugely busy seaport area.

Above from left:
Walls left in disrepair.

The entrance to the Pleasure Beach Ghost Town.

Abandoned buildings.

Opposite:
The restaurant in Pleasure Beach.

The bridge was built of wood and covered in creosote, which is used to preserve the wood, but is also extremely flammable; this was the community's biggest weakness and threat. There was an allocation of funds from the state to replace the bridge before the fire of 1996. However, the project never went through, either due to failure of the local government to follow up with the requirements for the project or because the state rescinded the appropriation due to cost-benefit analysis and couldn't justify the funds. Opinion seems to be divided between local government officials and local inhabitants.

The bridge fire that shut down Pleasure Beach was on Father's Day, in 1996 and there were a few hundred people on the island. Some were there for just a fun day on the beach, as Pleasure Beach was opened free of charge to anyone who wanted to visit. Others had come by to see a matinee performance of Neil Simon's *Laughter on the 23rd Floor* at the Polka Dot Playhouse. Also present were many of the town's residents who lived or vacationed in the forty-four cottages on the Stratford side of the island. When the residents saw the smoke billowing into the sky, they rushed to the bridge and their fears were realized. The bridge, the only access for motor vehicle traffic, was ablaze. On the mainland, the firefighters desperately tried to extinguish the fire, but their hoses couldn't reach the lower sections that were burning. They were also hampered by the wind that was blowing the fire away from the firefighters, toward the island.

While they fought on the mainland for control of the fire, the people on the island were not idle. A bucket brigade was formed to help douse the flames. Between the two sides, the fire was finally put out, but not before 200 feet of the center section of the bridge was destroyed. More than 180 vehicles were trapped, along with about 200 boats that could not pass due to the fire damaging the swing span that allowed the larger boats to pass into Long Island Sound. Eventually, most of the vehicles were ferried off the island and the way was cleared for the boats to make their escape. As for

the people on the island, they were stuck overnight until transport could be arranged to get them off the island.

The city claimed that the cost to repair the bridge would be 20 to 30 million dollars, although three years later, a new bridge was proposed at "only" 8 million dollars (12 million dollars less to start from scratch, which seems odd). It was decided by the town council, the day after the fire, that the resident's leases would not be renewed and the island would have to be vacated. When the residents tried to negotiate to purchase the land, they were refused. The city felt that without a bridge there was no way to protect the residents from fire or crime, since there was no way to get fire trucks or police cruisers to the residents.

Over the years, there had been interest expressed by Disney, in 1984, and Donald Trump, in 1987, to purchase the land from the towns and build an amusement park on the site; yet there appears to have been little effort to restore or make use of this incredibly valuable area.

In 2011, fifteen years after the fire, the desolated remains are still, mostly, standing. The 2 million dollar bathhouse that was never opened, since it had been completed just before the bridge burned, still sits on the beach, covered with graffiti and surrounded by beach on one side and the other, cracked-up pavement that once would have been a parking lot. The Playhouse still stands and you can see the remains of the carousel and the bumper car building that were mysteriously destroyed in 2009. Most of the cottages were removed in early 2011 – along with much of what had been left behind by the former residents of the town. It seems that every couple of years there are plans to revitalize, or at least make use of, the area, but, so far, it still remains abandoned. In 2012, the plans for the Bridgeport side of the island were to build a park for the public with playgrounds and swimming facilities. Stratford has plans to have walking trails through the area. Only time will tell if these plans will come to fruition.

Above from top:
The architecture, left to rot.

Open doorway, abandoned building.

Dilapidated carousel.

Right:
The remnants of an amusement ride on the midway.

AUTHOR NOTES

Not only is this the most modern of ghost towns we have visited, it is also the one that confuses me the most. I can't understand deserting this community. In New England, we have a lot of island communities. We have volunteer firefighters and neighborhood watches. If people are willing to live in an area and help keep each other safe, it can work out wonderfully. Also, Bridgeport has a busy waterfront area and ships can catch fire easily, especially if they are carrying hazardous cargo. The reasons just don't seem legitimate to abandon a multimillion dollar settlement. Beachfront property that isn't developed is a valuable commodity, and, even without the bridge, the area is accessible by boat or walking at low tide. So the questions remain, why was Pleasure Beach abandoned and why has it been left to sit for over fifteen years?

We visited Pleasure Beach on a warm October afternoon into evening. We hiked the two-plus miles to the town at low tide. The beach was littered with the oddments that were left behind when the cottages were hauled out of the area. It is eerie to walk down the beach and see abandoned children's toys, a damaged infant carrier, and even the ripped remains of an American flag. The town was chilling. The air had the feeling of an electric charge, and as we walked down the former streets, there was the constant feeling of being watched (which we probably were being watched, since I am sure there were homeless people staying in the dilapidated buildings). There was something deeply unsettling about walking around what is still very recognizable as a town and having the mixture of empty buildings, discarded household items, and buildings that have been destroyed along with the debris just lying strewn about the streets.

My co-author, Summer, described it as feeling as though you had been dropped into a zombie apocalypse story, and she was vocally anxious to leave. We checked out the bathhouse area and left via the precarious boardwalk; someone didn't want to walk back through town. As we started walking back to our car, we were serenaded by wild howls of the people hiding out in the town. Quite the send off.

~Cathy

Top row from left:
The no-longer-merry Merry-Go-Round.

The Polka Dot Playhouse, now covered in graffiti.

Handicap parking spaces outside of the restaurant.

Bottom row from left:
The gateway to the Pleasure Beach boardwalk.

Graffiti and overgrowth in the abandoned town of Pleasure Beach.

The deteriorating boardwalk.

36

SEPTEMBER 11ᵀᴴ MEMORIAL

Hudson, New Hampshire

Simple stones, without flair, stand as quiet reminders of a series of events that would change the way Americans looked at the world forever after.

8:46:26 – Flight 11 impacts the north tower of the World Trade Center

9:02:59 – Flight 75 impact the south tower of the World Trade Center

9:37:46 – Flight 77 impacts the western side of The Pentagon

9:59:04 – The south tower of the World Trade Center collapses

10:03:11 – Flight 95 crashes near Shanksville, Pennsylvania

10:28:25 – The north tower of the World Trade Center collapses

Less than two hours and nearly 3,000 lives taken.
Families lacking the closure of proper burials for their loved ones.
A country in grief, but a surge of patriotism that can only be obtained through shared experience and a desire to never forget the fallen.

A Fitting Tribute

When Hudson, New Hampshire, Fire Department Captain David Morin heard that the Port Authority of New York and New Jersey was undertaking a project to provide salvaged steel from the Twin Towers for memorials

Opposite:
The 9/11 Memorial at Benson Park in Hudson, New Hampshire. A father and daughter explore the site together.

to be erected in all fifty states, he immediately applied for a piece. He made a highly symbolic design from a rough sketch on a napkin, and spearheaded a committee to properly memorialize the tragic events.

The town was approved for a three- to five-foot piece, but when Captain Morin faxed a rendering of his design to the authorities, he received a phone call within fifteen minutes that he would receive a piece that would help realize the design. The following week, a volunteer crew drove a donated flatbed truck to John F. Kennedy Airport, retrieved a twenty-three-foot-tall beam that had been part of an elevator shaft in the north tower. Draped with an American flag, and amidst honks, waves, and salutes, the group returned to New Hampshire with their piece of history.

Dedicated on September 11, 2011, on the 10th anniversary of the tragedy, the memorial is highly representational. On a pentagonal-shaped base, and covered by lush grass that symbolizes the Pennsylvania field, the entrance to the memorial follows the flight path of Flight 77 into the Pentagon. A curved concrete pathway, which includes fragments of the material that was attached to the beam at the time of its retrieval, leads visitors to the upright beam and a glass tower fashioned in likeness of the World Trade Center. Stones along the pathway feature key moments in the timeline of the event, a breakdown of the demographics of those who perished and a request that we "Never Forget."

AUTHOR NOTES

We stopped at Benson Park as part of our travels on Memorial Day Weekend. The sun was shining and the sounds of children playing at the nearby playground added a grounding influence to the experience. Here, where you can literally reach out and touch the steel that crumbled in New York City, you are instantly taken back to that moment in time when you learned of what was happening and the dawning of the understanding that we were a nation at war. Simultaneously, however, the mothers pushing strollers, children riding bikes and picnicking families that surround the grounds bring a sharp reminder that our nation did not fall, has recovered, and continues to thrive. We are still the land of the free and the home of the brave, and terrorism has not won.

It bears noting how different this memorial is from others of its kind. Though the goal is clearly to educate the public and future generations about the tragedy, it does so in a way that does not promote fear. Walking the grounds, you will not see mention of Al-Queda, Osama Bin Laden, or even terrorism. The language engraved on the stones is thoughtfully planned and uses words like "impact" rather than "crash" or "explosion." I sincerely hope that others take note of the strength of these choices and follow a similar approach when designing future tributes, keeping the focus where it belongs: on people – and not places and atrocities.

~Summer

VISITORS' INFORMATION

The Hudson 9-11 Memorial is located in Benson Park, site of the former Benson's Wild Animal Farm, at 27 Kimball Road in Hudson, New Hampshire.

From left:
The twenty-three-foot beam that was once a part of an elevator shaft at the World Trade Center.

"Never Forget."

Key moments in the timeline of the tragic events are noted on small stones.

CONCLUSION

New England is full of wondrous sites for you to visit. We have had the greatest time wandering around the region visiting places we've known about all our lives, but also finding new sites we didn't know existed. During our travels, we have met so many colorful and warm people and have heard more tales than we'll ever be able to write about. We have included directions to all these locations with the hopes that you will be inspired to visit these areas and have some adventures of your own.

About Respect

We would like to emphasize the need for caution and respect for these places. Many have been damaged by visitors. These sites are not only fragile, but important, and we need to be caretakers, as well as visitors, or they won't be there for others to visit. Respect is the thing to remember above all else. Whether you are visiting a graveyard, a memorial, or a ghost town, think about the people represented and how their families would be impacted by your behavior.

There are ghost towns that we have not included (notably Bara Hack and Dudley Town) because there has been so much damage and so many people have been loud and disrespectful to the property that the owners no longer allow visitors. Please be sure to do your part in keeping remaining sites accessible for all to enjoy.

Best wishes and safe travels.

~Summer and Cathy

ABOUT THE AUTHORS

Summer Paradis is a true New Englander, through and through, who now calls Maine home. A school psychologist by day, she keeps busy chasing after her very active son, Jacob, by night. She reads anything and everything she can get her hands on, loves to write and take photographs, and enjoys the field of paranormal investigation.

Cathy McManus is a lifelong Mainer. When not busy working as a computer technician, she spends much of her free time wandering cemeteries and old houses throughout New England. She's an avid researcher and photographer.

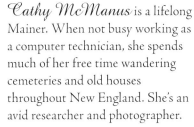

BIBLIOGRAPHY

BOOKS

Gellerman, Bruce and Erik Sherman. *Massachusetts Curiosities; Quirky Characters, Roadside Oddities, & Other Offbeat Stuff.* (Guilford, CT: The Globe Pequot Press, 2005)

Schmidt, Gary D. *Lizzie Bright and the Buckminster Boy.* (New York, NY: Clarion Books, 2004)

Morgan, Mark and Mark Sceurman. *Weird New England.* (New York, NY: Sterling Publishing Co., 2005)

Batignani, Karen Wentworth. *Maine's Coastal Cemeteries: A Historic Tour.* (Camden, ME: Down East Books, 2003)

Schlosser, S.E. *Spooky New England.* (Guilford, CT: The Globe Pequot Press, 2004)

McCain, Diana Ross. *Mysteries and Legends of New England: True Stories of the Unsolved and Unexplained.* (Guilford, CT: Morris Book Publishing, LLC, 2009)

Oliveri Schulte, Carol. *Ghosts on the Coast of Maine.* (Port Clyde, ME: Lone Maple Press, 1989)

Rogak, Lisa. *Stones and Bones of New England: A Guide to Unusual, Historic, and Otherwise Notable Cemeteries.* (Guilford, CT: The Globe Pequot Press, 2004)

Citro, Joseph A. and Diane E. Foulds. *Curious New England: The Unconventional Traveler's Guide To Eccentric Destinations.* (Lebanon, NH: University Press of New England, 2003)

Burnell, Alan and Kenny Wing. *Images of America: Lost Villages of Flagstaff Lake.* (Charleston, SC Arcadia Publishing 2010)

Former Relatives and Friends of the Dead River Valley, *Memories of Flagstaff, Dead River and Bigelow, There Was a Land.* (Augusta, ME J.S. McCarthy/Letter System Printers 3rd ed. 2004)

WEBSITES

capeannvacations.com/Vacation.cfm?id=8698&mk=37&ck=0&em=&ey= (accessed May 30, 2012)

Creepy Places of New England – Monson Center (accessed November 13, 2001)

http://blog.norsteel.com/2011/09/12/newhampshirecreateslarge911monument/ (accessed October 3, 2011)

http://collettemonuments.com/veterans.html (accessed December 2, 2011)

http://ctmonuments.net/2010/03/holocaustmemorialnewhaven/ (accessed July 19, 2012)

http://dallin.org/?page_id=674 (accessed June 23, 2012)

http://discovermagazine.com/1998/feb/lightelementsyan1410 (accessed April 30, 2012)

http://edhamiltonworks.com/amistad.htm (accessed July 26, 2012)

http://en.wikipedia.org/wiki/America%27s_Stonehenge (accessed April 30, 2012)

http://en.wikipedia.org/wiki/Daniel_Chester_French (accessed July 30, 2012)

http://en.wikipedia.org/wiki/Familiar_spirit (accessed July 3, 2012)

http://en.wikipedia.org/wiki/Gay_City_State_Park (accessed November 2, 2011)

http://en.wikipedia.org/wiki/General_Tom_Thumb (accessed May 29, 2012)

http://en.wikipedia.org/wiki/La_Amistad (accessed July 26, 2012)

http://en.wikipedia.org/wiki/Lewiston,_Maine (accessed June 29, 2012)

http://en.wikipedia.org/wiki/Lizzie_Bright_and_the_Buckminster_Boy (accessed November 1, 2011)

http://en.wikipedia.org/wiki/Malaga_Island (accessed November 1, 2011)

http://en.wikipedia.org/wiki/Massasoit (accessed June 23, 2012)

http://en.wikipedia.org/wiki/Newport,_Rhode_Island (accessed July 27, 2012)

http://en.wikipedia.org/wiki/P.T._Barnum (accessed May 29, 2012)

http://flickr.com/photos/schummi/sets/72157603231799666/ (accessed November 2, 2011)

http://ghosttowns.com/states/nh/monsonvillage.html (accessed October 3, 2011)

http://gravestonestudies.org/welcome.htm (accessed November 5, 2011)

http://library.brown.edu/omeka/exhibits/show/africanamericanprovidence/Hardscrabble (accessed May 1, 2012)

http://library.brown.edu/omeka/exhibits/show/africanamericanprovidence/SnowTown (accessed May 1, 2012)

http://myweb.northshore.edu/users/ccarlsen/poetry/gloucester/memorialshistory.htm

http://nativeamericanencyclopedia.com/massasoit15811661/ (accessed June 23, 2012)

http://patriot.net/~crouch/artj/riot.html (accessed May 1, 2012)

http://redmen.org/ (accessed June 23, 2012)

http://toonsames.com/a_Trevor%27s_Colums/2010/41410_buried.htm (accessed May 11, 2012)

http://trailsoffreedom.com/gaycitystatepark (accessed November 2, 2011)

http://youtu.be/bf7apehyg Stories From Stone: Africans in Colonial Rhode Island by Elizabeth Delude Dix (accessed 2005)

https://sites.google.com/site/nomisturm/fitzhughlane (accessed May 30, 2012)

iwalkedaudiotours.com/2011/04/iwalkedboston'sirishfaminememorial/ (accessed July 12, 2012)

query.nytimes.com/gst/fullpage.html?res=9E0DEEDA123FF933A05755C0A960958260&sec=&spon=&.shtml (accessed November 1, 2011)

vthaunts.blogspot.com/2010/11/blackagnesfinalrestingplaceofjohn.html (accessed July 2, 2012)

vthaunts.blogspot.com/2010/11/blackagnesfinalrestingplaceofjohn.html (accessed July 2, 2012)

www.barregranite.org/industry.html (accessed May 8, 2012)

www.bu.edu/bridge/archive/2002/0201/archaeology.htm (accessed April 30, 2012)

www.centralvt.com/web/hope/ (accessed May 8, 2012)

www.colonialcemetery.com/Home.htm (accessed June 1, 2012)

www.concordma.gov/pages/ConcordMA_CemeteryMin/2006%20Minutes/S00DD3E537/29/12

www.connecticutmag.com/Blogs/OnConnecticut/August2010/NoFunatPleasureBeach/ndex.php? (accessed July 2, 2012)

www.crossroad.to/Books/symbols1.html (accessed January 9, 2011)

www.ctghostseekers.net/Gay_City_State_Park.html (accessed November 2, 2011)

www.ctpost.com/news/article/LongBeachroadworkgetsunderway389525.php#photo117434 (accessed July 2, 2012)

www.deathreference.com/Bl!Ce/BuriedAlive.html (accessed May 11, 2012)

www.downeast.com/magazine/2009/october/flagstafffound (accessed July 2, 2012)

www.en.wikipedia.org/wiki/Monument_Square_(Portland_Maine) (accessed December 2, 2011)

www.findagrave.com/cgibin/fg.cgi?page=gr&GRid=29912267 7/2/12 www.forestsociety.org/ourproperties/ (accessed September 9, 2011)

www.ghosttowns.com/states/ct/gaycity.html (accessed October 5, 2011)

www.ghostvillage.com/legends/2004/legends34_08012004.shtml (accessed April 30, 2012)

www.graveaddiction.com/greenmtvt.html (accessed May 9, 2012)

www.historyplace.com/worldhistory/famine/ 7/12/12 Television/Film: Creepy Places of New England: African Colonial Cemetery (accessed May 5, 2010)

www.mainememory.net/artifact/8795 (accessed December 2, 2011)

www.mcht.org/preserves/malagaisland.

www.montpeliervt.org (accessed May 9, 2012)

www.nashuatelegraph.com/news/931448196/worldtradecenterbeaminstalledathudson.html (accessed July 27, 2012)

www.necn.com/09/10/11/NHtowntounveilmonumenttoall911at/landing_newengland.html?&apID=5ec16af2fd564ef58845d3f6a41d0ac1 (accessed October 3, 2011)

www.nps.gov/boaf/historyculture/amh.htm (accessed November 22, 2011)

www.nps.gov/boaf/historyculture/shaw.htm (accessed November 22, 2011)

www.nps.gov/boaf/planyourvisit/things2do.htm (accessed November 22, 2011)

www.nps.gov/bost/historyculture/bhm.htm (accessed November 22, 2011)

www.nps.gov/bost/historyculture/bhm.htm (accessed May 30, 2012)

www.nps.gov/bost/historyculture/onc.htm (accessed November 22, 2011)

www.nps.gov/long/index.htm (accessed November 22, 2011)

www.nps.gov/mima/planyourvisit/placesstogo.htm (accessed November 22, 2011)

www.nps.gov/nr/travel/maritime/glo.htm (accessed May 30, 2012)

www.nps.gov/rowi/faqs.htm (accessed October 3, 2011)

www.nytimes.com/1988/03/06/nyregion/plantorevivepleasurebeach.html (accessed July 2, 2012)

www.portlandlandmarks.org/images/advocacy (accessed December 2, 2011)

www.profootballhof.com/history/stats/thanksgiving.aspx (accessed June 9, 2012)

www.roadsideamerica.com/tip/6736 (accessed May 25, 2012)

www.rootsweb.ancestry.com/~memoca/moca.htm (accessed November 5, 2011)

www.salemweb.com/memorial/ (accessed May 11, 2012)

www.salemweb.com/memorial/memorial.shtml (accessed May 11, 2012)

www.savepleasurebeach.com (accessed July 2, 2012)

www.stonehengeusa.com/ (accessed April 30, 2012)

www.thefreedomtrail.org/visitor/bunkerhill.html (accessed May 30, 2012)

www.thefreedomtrail.org/visitor/bunkerhill.html (accessed November 22, 2011)

www.uaine.org/ (accessed May 25, 2012)

www.vermonter.com/hopecemetery.asp (accessed May 11, 2012)

www.wmur.com/print/29133394/detail.htm (accessed October 3, 2011)

www.youtube.com/watch?v=YcWRq99IGVc

OTHER SOURCES

"Artist Duca dies leaving legacy of joy." *Gloucester Daily Times* pp. A1 & A9, January 17, 1997

"Remember The Lost." *New Haven Register*, May 25, 2012

"Unveiling of Lane Statue will complete sculptor's Work." *Gloucester Daily Times* pp A1 & A7, August 28, 1997

124th Legislature, Second Regular Session. State of Maine House of Representatives. Supplement No. 20 Joint Resolution Recognizing The Tragic Expulsion Of The Residents of Malaga Island, Maine in 1912 And Redirecting Ourselves To The Maine Ideals of Tolerance, Independence and Equality For All Peoples, April, 7, 2010

Balliett, Jamie Fargo. "Waterbury's Ricker Cemetery." *The Newsletter of the Vermont Old Cemetery Association*, Summer 2000

Connecticut Department of Energy and Environmental Protection. Gay City State Park, 2011. Marlborough, CT: Gay City State Park, Hebron, CT, 2011.

Connecticut Department of Energy and Environmental Protection. The Geology of Gay City State Park, 2011. Marlborough, CT: Gay City State Park, Hebron, CT, 2011.

Dubrule, Deborah. "Malaga Revisited: On a Casco Bay Island, a Shameful Incident in Maine's History Comes To Light" *The Working Waterfront*, Aug. 1, 2005

Edition. Concord, MA: Friends of Minute Man National Park, Concord, MA, 2010.

Englenardt, Stanley L. "Channel One: Turning on Turned-Off Teenagers." *Reader's Digest* pp 2934)

Fishell, Darren. "Reconciliation Reigns on Malaga Island." *The Times Record*, Sept. 13, 2010

Hartill, Daniel. "Veteran Memorial Park: 4,365 Names and Growing." *The Sun Journal*, Nov. 8, 2010

Koenig, Seth. "Malaga Island's Place In Maine History Preserved." *The Times Record*, August 18, 2009

Long, Tom, Alfred M. Duca, 76 sculptor and pioneer in painting process. *Boston Globe*, obituaries, January 17, 1997

Maguire, John. "Malaga Island's History Revisited at Descendants' Gathering." *The Coastal Journal*, Sept. 29, 2011

Malaga Island Preserve, Phippsburg, Maine. *Malaga Island – An Overview of its Natural and Cultural History*, 2011. Topsham, ME: Maine Coast Heritage Trust, 2011.

Malaga Island Preserve, Phippsburg, Maine. Malaga Island Preserve Map, 2011. Topsham, ME: Maine Coast Heritage Trust, 2011.

National Park Service, U.S. Department of the Interior. "What? No Elevator? And Other Facts About Bunker Hill Monument." Boston, MA: Bunker Hill Monument, Boston National Historical Park, Boston, MA, 2011.

National Park Service, U.S. Department of the Interior. *The Minute Man Messenger*, 2010

Nemitz, Bill. "After 98 Years, An Apology Long Overdue." *The Portland Press Herald*, Sept. 10, 2010

Nickell, Joe. "Entombed Alive!" *Investigative Files*, Volume 32.2, March/April 2008

Pushkar, R.G. "The Tapestry of his life." *Boston Globe* p. 18, August 12, 1985)

Sanders, Alexandra. "Trip To The New Haven Holocaust Memorial Helps Students." *New Haven Register*, May 25, 2012

Slover, Daryn. "Honoring Their Service." *The Sun Journal*, July 30, 2004

Vermont Agency of Natural Resources, Department of Forests, Parks and Recreation. Little River State Park Map and Guide, 2011. Waterbury, VT: Little River State Park, Waterbury, VT, 2011.

Vermont Agency of Natural Resources, Department of Forests, Parks and Recreation. Little River State Park History Hike, 2011. Waterbury, VT: Little River State Park, Waterbury, VT, 2011.

Wheeler, Kitty. "Malaga Island To Mark Shameful Centennial in 2012." *The Coastal Journal*, Aug. 11, 2010

Woodward, Colin. "A Quiet Apology." *Downeast Magazine*, Aug. 2011

PERSONAL INTERVIEW

Dickerman, Russ. May 27, 2012

INDEX

126